THE URINARY SEDIMENT

THE URINARY SEDIMENT

An integrated view

G.B. Fogazzi,
P. Passerini,
C. Ponticelli and
E. Ritz

With an introduction by
J.S. Cameron

CHAPMAN & HALL MEDICAL

London · Glasgow · Weinheim · New York · Tokyo · Melbourne · Madras

Published by Chapman & Hall, 2-6 Boundary Row, London SE1 8HN, UK

Chapman & Hall, 2-6 Boundary Row, London SE1 8HN, UK

Blackie Academic & Professional, Wester Cleddens Road, Bishopbriggs, Glasgow G64 2NZ, UK

Chapman & Hall GmbH, Pappelallee 3, 69469 Weinheim, Germany

Chapman & Hall Inc., One Penn Plaza, 41st Floor, New York, NY10119, USA

Chapman & Hall Japan, Thomson Publishing Japan, Hirakawacho Nemoto Building, 6F, 1-7-11 Hirakawa-cho, Chiyoda-ku, Tokyo 102, Japan

Chapman & Hall Australia, Thomas Nelson Australia, 102 Dodds Street, South Melbourne, Victoria 3205, Australia

Chapman & Hall India, R. Seshadri, 32 Second Main Road, CIT East, Madras 600 035, India

This edition 1994

© 1994 Masson S.p.A.

This edition not for sale in Italy, Spain or Spanish-speaking countries

Original edition — *The Urinary Sediment* — © 1993 Masson S.p.A.

Printed in Hong Kong by Thomas Nelson

ISBN 0 412 59300 0

Authors

G.B. Fogazzi,   Senior assistant, Division of Nephrology
and Dialysis, Ospedale Maggiore, IRCCS, Milano, Italy.

P. Passerini,   Assistant, Division of Nephrology and Dialysis,
Ospedale Maggiore, IRCCS, Milano, Italy.

C. Ponticelli,   Director, Division of Nephrology and Dialysis,
Ospedale Maggiore, IRCCS, Milano, Italy.

E. Ritz,   Head, Renal Unit, Department of Internal Medicine,
Ruperto Carola University, Heidelberg, Germany.

J.S. Cameron,   Professor of Renal Medicine,
Guy's Campus, United Medical and Dental School,
London, United Kingdom.

This book is dedicated to the memory of our friend
and colleague doctor Stefano Casati.

Contents

Chapter 4.

Introduction

"When the patient dies the kidneys may go to the pathologist, but while he lives the urine is ours. It can provide us day by day, month by month, and year by year with a serial story of the major events within the kidney. The examination of the urine is the most essential part of the physical examination of any patient..." (Thomas Addis, 1948 [1]).

Doctors have been looking at the urine for diagnostic information for at least two and a half milennia [2], because examination of the urine was already part of the Hippocratic system. However, for the first thousand years or more this enquiry was pursued by eye, unaided either by microscopy or chemistry (Figure 1).

This new textbook and atlas on the urinary sediment reflect a renewed interest in microscopy of the urine in recent years, after a period of relative neglect since the days when Addis wrote. One clue to the origins of that temporary neglect is given in the quotation: "when the patient dies his kidneys may go to the pathologist...". Addis wrote just after Alwall had unsuccessfully attempted to add renal biopsy to autopsy [3], and just before its successful application by Brun [4], and Muehrcke and Kark [5]. In the excitement of actually following renal histology during life, many clinicians — myself included — partially forgot the powerful lessons the urine can teach us.

This has happened before. In 1844, Golding Bird — yet another of the amazing run of Guy's physicians on the mid 19th Century — writes [6] of the "rediscovery" of the art of microscoping the urine. He was referring to the fact that after the assembly of the first simple microscopes in the 16th century and compound microscopes in the early 17th, urine was examined by observers as early as de Peiresc in 1580, who described urinary crystals resembling "a heap of rhomboidal bricks" [7]. This may well be the first record of urine microscopy, but despite the continuing popularity of divinative uroscopy [2] (Figure 1) it was not until about the time of the first microscopic observations of kidney tissue itself [8, 9] in the late 1830s that observers began to examine the urine by the microscope with any regularity. This may have been the result of better objectives about this time (see below).

Although bloody urine had been noted in scarlatinal nephritis throughout the 17th and 18th centuries [10-12], most notably by the astute Swedish paediatrician Rosén von Rosenstein [13], I have been unable to find any record during this period of the confirmation of the presence of red cells in the urine by microscopy; that may come as a result of further enquiry. Neither Cotugno [14] (Figure 2) who discovered and named albuminuria in the 1770s, nor Bright and Bostock, although they made many chemical observations on their patients [15] used a microscope on the urine, although by 1840 Bright's student Toynbee was microdissecting kidneys and examining them microscopically [16]. Interestingly, William Bowman himself — although he made no microscopical observations on the urine — clearly appreciated that red cells could pass through the Malpighian corpuscles in disease. He describes, in a footnote to his classic paper of 1842, kidneys from patients with Bright's disease that he examined [17, pp. 67-8]: "It is well known that blood is often passed in the urine during the course of the disease, especially at the earlier periods of it, when many circumstances contribute to prove that the kidneys are in a state of sanguineous turgescence. How does this blood escape into the ducts of the gland? The organ examined at this time presents on its surface and throughout its cortical substance, scattered red dots, of somewhat irregular shape, not accurately rounded, and generally as large as pins' heads, that is very many times larger than

Fig. 1. *Uroscopy was one of the most important aspects of patient investigation in the past. This was based on the consideration that changes in the mixture of body fluids ("humores") should be reflected in changes of the color, turbidity and sediment of the urine. (Avicenna, Canon, Glasgow, Hunter, MS 9, Folio 84; from Bleker, J. "Die Geschichte der Nierenkrankheiten", Boehringer Mannheim GmbH, 1972. Used with permission).*

the Malpighian bodies... they are nothing less than *the convolutions of the tube filled with blood* (author's italics) that has burst into it from the gorged Malpighian tuft at its extremity". However it seems credit must be given to the founder of French nephrology, Pierre Rayer (1793-1867) for the introduction of regular urine microscopy to clinical practice. In the preface of his magnificent *Traité des maladies des reins* published in three volumes between 1839 and 1841 [18], he writes: "It is to be regretted that another method of investigation, microscopical examination, is not yet generally employed to examine the matter suspended in the urine, thrown down by cooling, or which one may precipitate by various reagents... I cannot thus understand the lack of urgency in the majority of physicians to avail themselves of the microscope in the examination of the urine".

As Richet recently expressed it "la microscopie de l'urine, en revanche, fut crée par Rayer lui-même" [19] and he notes that Rayer made a microscope available at all hours for his junior associates to microscope the urine. Rayer examined and analysed the crystals present in the urine, as many had before him, but — and this was new — he noted also the red cells, the pus cells, the epithelial cells, fatty bodies and sperm. He realised that otherwise normal (clear) urine might nevertheless contain an excess of red cells — the first description of microscopic haematuria.

Thus in 1841, in his classic book on albuminuria, Alfred Becquerel could casually refer [20] to "examen microscopique" of the urine: and notes again that in perfectly clear urine, one sees only sheets of epithelium, in urine with mucus, globules of this substance, closely resembling globules of pus, and also red blood cells "plus souvent déformés et irreguliers" — the first description of dysmorphic red cells? He noted also sperm, and of course crystals: calcium and magnesium carbonate, and phosphates, including ammonium magnesium phosphate. Animal chemistry had developed rapidly since the beginning of the 19th century [21] and the chemical approach to disease was being applied in many centres throughout Europe.

DOMINICI COTUNNII

PHIL. ET MED. DOCT.

D E

ISCHIADE
NERVOSA

COMMENTARIUS.

V E N E T I I S,
MDCCLXXXII.

TYPIS BARTHOLOMAEI OCCHI
SUPERIORUM PERMISSU.

Fig. 2. *Domenico Cotugno (1736-1780) a Pugliese who became physician to the Royal house of Naples and Sicily, and who in 1774 made the first description of albuminuria. He introduced this term because of the resemblance between the coagulum obtained on heating the urine of a dropsical soldier who was probably suffering from malarial nephropathy ("Ovi albuminis persimilem") and coagulated egg-white. However, Cotugno made no observations on the urinary deposit. His notes on coagulable urine were published on a book on the sciatic nerve because Cotugno was interested in coagulation of body fluids, including cerebrospinal fluid. As is well known, Cotugno completely misinterpreted the significance of the appearance of albumin in the urine, regarding it as a favorable sign, which represented the excretion of the (coagulable) oedema fluid! (Wellcome Historical Library, London).*

Two years later in Germany, Jacob Henle [22] recognized the urinary tubular casts seen in histological sections as identical to those found in the urine; Frerichs, writing in 1851, also credits a physician named Nasse [23] as reporting them at the same time. The previous year both Scherer [24] and Franz Simon [25] described casts in the urine, possibly for the first time, and this observation was so striking that Golding Bird reproduces the illustration of them in his own book [6] *Urinary deposits. Their diagnosis, pathology and therapeutical indications*, published in 1844, following a paper on the subject in Guys' Hospital reports of 1843 [26] which indicates he had been studying the urinary sediment for some time. This was the first comprehensive description of the presence and significance of urinary crystals and sediments, which ran to three English and two American editions over the next decade, and placed urine microscopy firmly into the realm of routine clinical examination. Curiously, Frerichs does not mention it.

Bird notes that his copy of Simon's picture (Figure 3) is "the common appearance of deposits in the urine of morbus Brightii" and that "a tubular mass of coagulated albumen, probably the cast of a uriniferous tubule, entangling granules and blood discs, occupies the centre of the figure". Present also are red cells, epithelial cells, and "large organic globules" which contain "nuclei" (although not cell nuclei). I am unsure what these particles may represent in con-

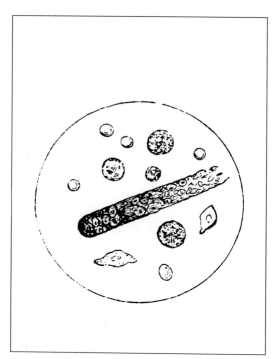

Fig. 3. *One of the earliest illustrations of a uri-nary cast, taken from Simon's paper of 1843 [25] and reproduced in the first edition of Golding Bird's book [6] the following year (see the text).*

Fig. 4(a). *Normal red cells in fresh urine; from Golding Bird [6]. Rouleaux are still present.*

Fig. 4(b). *Altered red cells in urine. Bird thought that this appearance resulted from the urine standing for a while in the bladder or in the urine jar (see the text). Today we might think different-ly.*

Fig. 3

Fig. 4(a)   Fig. 4(b)

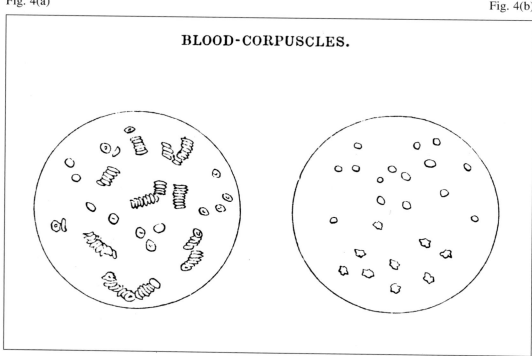

BLOOD-CORPUSCLES.

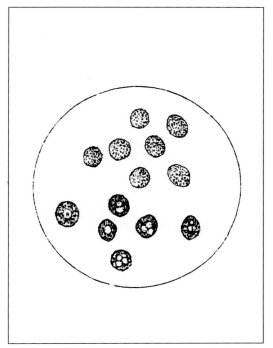

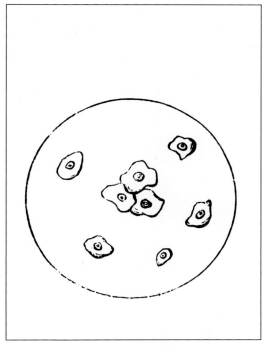

Fig. 5. *Pus cells as illustrated by Bird [6]. Again these had been observed and correctly identified by Rayer [18].*

Fig. 6. *Epithelial cells in the urine, from Bird (1844) [6]. These had been observed by previous microscopists, including Rayer in 1839 [18] and Becquerel in 1841 [20].*

temporary terms. Golding Bird also illustrates fresh blood in the urine (Figure 4(a)), with round cells and rouleaux, which he contrasts with older bleeding, some of the dispersed cells in 4(b) showing clear evidence of membrane "spikes" and "hooks" of the type illustrated using electron microscopy recently [27, and see page 30]. Bird tells us that he ordinarily used "a good achromatic objective of a quarter of an inch (6 mm) focus", but that one of one seventh (3.6 mm) or one eighth (3.2 mm) focus was occasionally used. Richet [19] notes that the achromatic lens was perfected by C.L. Chevalier (1804-1850) in Paris, and probably both Rayer and Bird depended upon this advance for their ability to describe the urinary sediment with accuracy. Bird shows also pus cells (Figure 5) and epithelial cells (Figure 6).

In the later editions of his book, Bird refers to the important work of George Johnson [28] on fatty deposits in the urine, published in 1846. Although it was known that the kidneys of nephrotics contain an excess of fat [8, 9], Johnson was unaware of these papers; and when he demonstrated fat in nephrotic kidneys as well as an excess of fat both microscopically (Figure 7) and chemically in both epithelial cells and casts contained in the urine, he claimed this as an original observation; when he presented this work to the Medical Chirurgical Society in London in 1845 he was tartly reprimanded by an anonymous correspondent in the Lancet [29], who used the pseudonym "One who reads before he "discovers"", drawing his attention to the prior publications from the Continent [8, 9]. The idea of a fatty degenerative parenchymatous nephritis gained strength from Munk's use of polarised light on the urinary sediment for the first time in 1913 [30], showing the beautiful and now familiar "Achsenkreuz" of the fatty casts in the urine (Figure 8); these observations led to the term "lipoid nephrosis" which

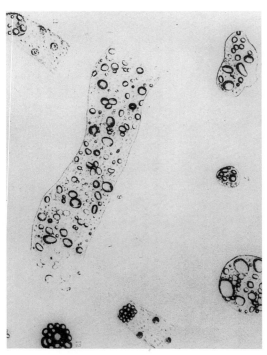

Fig. 7. *The urinary sediment as illustrated in Johnson's article of 1846 [28]. He drew attention to the fatty (oily) casts, (top and bottom) in the urine of nephrotic patients (mag X 400) and noted that this corresponded to fatty deposits in the renal tubule, seen in an unstained, isolated tubule in the centre of the picture.*

Fig. 8. *An illustration from Munk's paper of 1913 [30]. Polarised light was used for the first time to show the presence of lipid.*

Fig. 7

Fig. 8

Nachweis fettähnlicher Substanzen, der sog. Lipoide, im Urin.

Diese Lipoide erweisen sich im polarisierten Lichte im Gegensatz zu dem isotropen Neutralfett als doppeltbrechend. Während eine Unterscheidung im gewöhnlichen Lichte nur sehr schwer möglich ist, beobachtet man die Lipoide im Polarisationsmikroskop als feine Tröpfchen mit einem schwarzen Axenkreuz und 4 hellaufleuchtenden Segmenten, so dass sie wie helle Sternchen erscheinen, die Neutralfetttröpfchen sind dagegen im polarisierten Lichte nicht sichtbar (s. Fig. 1). Schon vor

Lipoiddruse.   Lipoidzylinder.   Gewebsfetzen mit Lipoid.

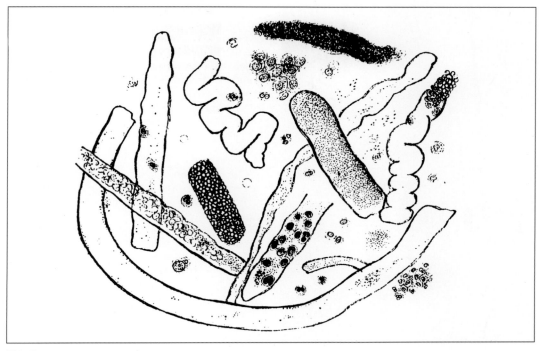

Fig. 9

Fig. 10

Fig. 9. *Urinary sediment in a fatal case of nephritis illustrated in Rieder's atlas of the urinary sediment, published at the end of the 19th Century [32]. The original caption reads: "contracted kidney with fatal outcome. Hyaline cylinders, covered with numerous globules of albumin, thus seeming fragmented, cylinders with fatty droplets, cells with fatty globules, partly free and partly enclosed in the cylinders, innumerable scattered globules of albumin".*

Fig. 10. *Rieder's illustration of red cells in the urine; again as in Bird's work, there is awareness of the fact that some red cells may be grossly dysmorphic in haematuric patients (see text for Rieder's description of these appearances).*

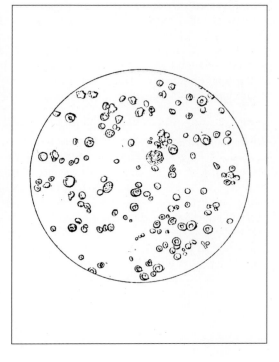

Fig. 11. *Thomas Addis (1881-1949), who through-out his career emphasised the value of examining and quantitating the urinary sediment in glomeru-lonephritis. He felt strongly that morphological, rather than functional, aspects of renal diseases needed emphasis [33]. He pointed to the signifi-cance of broad, "renal failure" casts [36], al-though noting that they had been described previ-ously as early as 1868, by Wyss. In this 1925 ar-ticle Addis writes: "It is an index of the preoccu-pation of clinical investigators with functional measures to the exclusion of methods of morphol-ogy, and their quite unwarranted faith in the dic-tum of Schlayer and others to the effect that little or nothing can be learned from the microscopic examination of the urine". (The photograph of Thomas Addis, reproduced from Peitzman S.J.: Kidney Int. 37. 833-40, 1990, was provided by the Lane Medical Archives, Stanford University Med-ical Center. Used with permission).*

remained current until the 1970s.

The idea of microscopic examination of the urine as a useful tool was not accepted immedi-ately however. Owen Rees, one of Bright's pupils at Guy's and an experienced researcher and student of renal physiology and medicine, wrote in 1843 [31]: "it may appear how we occa-sionally possess means of proving on large masses the views to which we have been led by microscopic examination — a method of enquiry which, valuable as it certainly is, must al-ways be received with the distrust naturally felt towards a means of investigation so tempting to the imagination and which, it is to be feared, has already been productive of much mischief in the hands of the ingenious and unscrupulous". I do not know to which spurious research he is referring!

Thus throughout the next century until the introduction of renal biopsy examination of the urine was the main route in life by which the nature and activity of the disease could be judged. Thus in 1898, Herman Rieder [32] published beautiful illustrations of casts in his At-las of clinical microscopy of the urine (Figure 9), and most interestingly noted: "in renal bleeding... (the erythrocytes) differ greatly in both size and shape, some being small and con-tracted whilst others look like a thorn apple. At times (the erythrocytes) are swollen, deprived of their pigment... or they are dismantled in granules or spheres containing haemoglobin (Fig-ure 10)".

The study of the urinary sediment reached its apotheosis in the studies of Thomas Addis (Fig-ure 11) [33] quoted at the head of this introduction. For more than two decades he examined the urine of countless patients with all varieties of renal diseases and noted their appearances; for the first time photographs of the urinary sediment are used to illustrate the articles. He was suspicious of functional analysis of the kidney, preferring as he put it, the tradition epitomised by the book of Volhard and Fahr; nevertheless he advocated quantitation of both the urinary sediment in a concentrated acid overnight urine, and quantitation of proteinuria.

Addis would have been delighted by the fact that today we have added even more technical advances to the examination of the urinary sediment. Phase contrast microscopy [34] allows us to see the altered red cells of renal bleeding more easily, although their origin remains a subject for vigorous debate (see pages 24), and monoclonal antibodies allow us to phenotype the white blood cells in the urine [35], or to examine the expression of HLA antigens or adhesion molecules on the shed tubular epithelial cells.

However, we return always to the simple optical microscopy of our ancestors for most of our work, allowing the urine to present to us day-by-day, free and easily accessible, a sample of what is happening in the kidney and the urinary tract. This book tells us, beautifully and lucidly, what we can learn from that examination.

J. Stewart Cameron
Guy's Hospital, London UK

Acknowledgement:

I am grateful to Professors Fine, Ritz and Fogazzi for valuable help in preparing this manuscript.

References

[1] ADDIS T.: *Glomerular nephritis. Diagnosis and treatment*. Chapter 1. New York, Macmillan, 1948.

[2] FINE L.: *Circle of urine glasses: art of uroscopy*. Am. J. Nephrol. 6: 307-11, 1986.

[3] ALWALL N.: *On the organization of treatment with the artificial kidney and clinical Nephrology in the 1940s and following decades. A contribution to the history of medicine*. I The nineteen-forties. Dialysis. Transpl. 9: 307-11, 1980.

[4] IVERSEN P., BRUN C.: *Aspiration biopsy of the kidney*. Am. J. Med. 11: 324-30, 1951.

[5] MUEHRCKE R.C., KARK R.M., PIRANI C.L.: *Technique of percutaneous kidney biopsy in the prone position*. J. Urol. 74: 267-77, 1955.

[6] BIRD G.: *Urinary deposits. Their diagnosis, pathology, and therapeutical indications*. London, Churchill (1st edition), 1844.

[7] VAN SWIETEN J.: *Commentarius*. Edinburgh 1776. XVI, p. 81. (Van Swieten quotes Gassendi as writing that Peiresc microscoped the urine around 1580).

[8] VALENTIN G.: *Repertorium für Anatomie und Physiologie*. Bern und St. Gall., Huber, 11(2), pp. 290-1, 1837.

[9] GLUGE G. *Anatomisch-microskopische Untersuchung zur allgemeinen und speziellen Pathologie*. Jena, II, 126-131, 1842.

[10] STORCH J.: *Praktischer und theoretischer Traktat vom Scharlachfieber*. Gotha, C. Mevius, pp. 238-42, 1742.

[11] NAVIER P.T.: *Dissertation en forme de lettres sur plusieurs maladies populaires qui ont regné a Châlons sur Marne*. Paris, Cavelier, pp. 308, 438, 1753.

[12] REIL J. Ch.: *Über die Erkentniss und Cur der Fieber*. Halle, Curshe Buchhandlung, bk 5, pp. 123-5, 1799-1815.

[13] ROSÉN VON ROSENSTEIN N.: *Underratleser on bjarnsjukdomar och deras botmedel*. Stockholm 1765. (Translated into English by Sparrman A., London T. Cadel., pp. 158-9, 1776).

[14] COTUGNO D.: *De ischiade nervosa commentarius*. Vienna, Graeffer, 1778.

[15] BRIGHT R.: *Reports of medical cases etc*. London, Longman, 1827.

[16] CAMERON J.S., BECKER E.L.: *Richard Bright and observations in renal histology*. Guy's Hosp. Rep., 114: 159-71, 1964.

[17] BOWMAN W.: *On the structure and use of the Malpighian bodies of the kidney with observations on the circulation through that gland*. Phil. Trans. Roy Soc. Lond. 132: 57-80, 1842.

[18] RAYER P.F.O.: *Traité des maladies des reins, etc*. 3 vols and Atlas. Paris, J.B. Balliere, 1839-41. Preface, pp. VIII-IX; and pp. 58, 99, 105, 114, 116-7, 122, 207.

[19] RICHET G. *Pierre Rayer, createur de la méthodologie néphrologique*. Histoire des Sciences Medicales 25: 285-92, 1991.

[20] BECQUEREL A.: *Séméiotique des urines; ou traité des altérations des urines dans les maladies; suivi d'un traité de la maladie de Bright au divers ages de la vie*. Paris, Fortin et Masson, p. 172, 1841.

[21] BROCK W.H.: *The life and work of Wiliam Prout*. Med. Hist. 9: 101-26, 1965.

[22] HENLE F.G.J. In: Pfeufer C. *Morbus Bright*. Klinische Mitteilungen. Z. Nat. Med. 1: 57-60, 1844. This article includes a note by Henle on pp. 60-61, in which he describes casts).

[23] NASSE: *Schmidt's Jahrbucher*, 356, 1843. Quoted in: Frerichs F.T. *Die Bright'sche Neirenkrankheit und deren Behandlung*. Braunschweig, Bieweg., p. 9.

[24] SCHERER: *Chemische und mikroskopische Untersuchungen*. Heidelberg, ibid., p. 9, 1843.

[25] SIMON J.F.: *Beitrage zur physiologisch und pathologische Chemie und Microskopie*. Berlin, 1843. B.s 190; *see also: Ueber eigentumliche Formen in Harsedmiment bei Morbus Bright*. Arch. Anat. Physiol. Wissenschaft. Med. 28-30, 1843.

[26] BIRD G.: *Note on the microscopic globules found in the urine*. Guy's Hosp. Rep., 7: 336-40, 1842.

[27] BIRCH D.F., FAIRLEY K.F., WHITWORTH J.A., et al.: *Urinary erythrocyte morphology in the diagnosis of glomerular hematuria*. Clin. Nephrol. 20: 78-84, 1983.

[28] JOHNSON G.: *On the minute anatomy and pathology of Bright's disease of the kidney and on the relation of the renal disease to those diseases of the liver, heart and arteries with which it is associated*. Med. Chir. Trans., 29: 1-43, 1846.

[29] *One who reads before he "discovers". On granular degeneration of the kidneys*. Lancet 1: 239 (letter), 1846.

[30] MUNK F.: *Klinische Diagnostik der degenerativen Nierenkrankungen*. Klin. Med. 78: 1-52, 1913.

[31] REES O.: *Observations on the blood, with reference to its peculiar condition in the morbus Brightii*. Guy's Hosp. Rep. 1 (NS): 317-29, 1843.

[32] RIEDER H.: *Atlas der klinischen Mikroscopie des Harnes*. Leipzig, Vogel, 1898.

[33] PEITZMAN S.J.: *Thomas Addis (1881-1949): mixing patients, rats and politics*. Kidney Int. 37: 833-40, 1990.

[34] BIRCH D.F., FAIRLEY K.F.: *Haematuria-glomerular or non-glomerular?* Lancet 2: 845-6, 1979.

[35] SEGASOTHY M., BIRCH D.F., FAIRLEY K.F., et al.: *Urine cytologic profile in renal allograft recipients determined by monoclonal antibodies*. Transplantation 47: 482-7, 1989.

[36] ADDIS T.: *Renal failure casts*. JAMA 84: 1013-5, 1925.

Chapter 1

Preparation and interpretation
of the urinary sediment

Urine collection

The procedure is most sensitive when morning urine, which is usually more concentrated and acidic, is examined. In outpatient clinics, one usually has urine voided at the moment to study. One should make sure that the patient has not been doing strenuous physical exercise and that he or she is afebrile. It is preferable to examine the patient while he or she is not undergoing excessive diuresis, since in diluted urine several types of elements of the urinary sediment are reduced in number in the aliquot centrifuged. Cellular elements especially may be partially or completely lysed. It is also undesirable to examine highly alkaline urine. Amorphous phosphate precipitates at high pH masking cellular elements. A high urine pH may also lead to lysis of casts [1].

In order to minimize contamination, the midstream urine technique is recommended. This implies that the first portion of the urine is discarded, since it may be contaminated with cellular elements and bacteria from the external urinary tract and genital area. However, the very first portion of the urine may be of diagnostic interest, when urethral disorders are suspected. Comparison of the first voided portion and the midstream portion of urine may distinguish between urethral and bladder infection.

If possible, the urine sediment should not be examined during menstruation, since contamination by erythrocytes is very likely. When there is doubt about contamination, or if contamination cannot be avoided, suprapubic puncture of the bladder should be considered (figure 1.1). If properly done, this procedure causes minimal discomfort and is safe. In contrast, bladder catheterization is not bacteriologically safe, may cause erythrocyturia in itself [2], and should be avoided.

Plastic bags attached to clean genitalia may be used for infants and small children who are unable to control micturition. If properly handled, adequate urine samples can be obtained, but there may be fecal contamination and spurious bacteriuria and one may still have to resort to suprapubic puncture.

Handling of urine

To avoid contamination upon standing, urine should be collected and transported in clean disposable plastic containers with a cover. The following pieces of equipment are necessary for evaluation of the urine:
— devices to measure urinary pH and osmolality (or specific gravity)
— graduated transparent containers to measure urine volume
— transparent graduated centrifuge tubes with conical bottoms
— a low speed centrifuge, well balanced to avoid vibrations
— a suction pump
— a Pasteur pipette or an automatic pipette

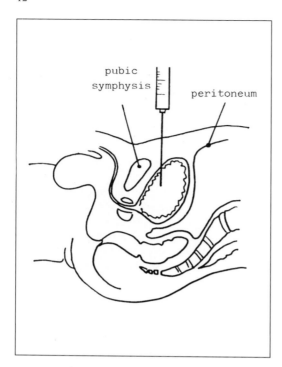

Fig. 1.1 *Suprapubic bladder punction.*
Patient in supine position with full bladder and a small pubic area shaved.
A 3$^1/_2$ inch 22-gauge spinal needle attached to a syringe.
Slow introduction of the needle at right angle through the skin just above the pubic symphysis, then quickly piercing the bladder and aspirating the urine.

— grease-free slides and cover slips
— a microscope, preferably a phase contrast microscope.
At least at the time of the first examination the urinary sediment should be evaluated by the nephrologist or by the physician in charge of the patient. Evaluation should be done as quickly as possible. This will avoid (i) bacterial overgrowth, (ii) the resulting enzymatic degradation of urea with ensuing alkalinization of the urine and the attendant risk of dissolution of casts and cells, as well as (iii) contamination from the air. Addition of formaldehyde, thymol, chloroform or thimerosal [3] has been recommended, but these are definitely inferior to prompt examination and should be used only if this option is not available. We discourage storing the samples in the refrigerator, since phosphates and urates precipitate at low temperature and heavy precipitation may mask diagnostically important elements of the urinary sediment.

Inspection

Macroscopic inspection of the urine reveals turbidity (which is of no diagnostic relevance in itself unless it is due to leucocyturia, seen by microscopy), macrohematuria and pigmenturia. While macrohematuria and the various types of pigmenturia can be differentiated by microscopic examination, it is useful to consider the causes of abnormal color of the urine, reported in tables 1.1 and 1.2.

Table 1.1 Different causes of pigmenturia

Endogenous factors	*Exogenous factors*
— hemoglobin	— vegetable pigments
— myoglobin	— alimentary pigments
— porphirins	— drugs
— alkaptonuria	— chemicals
— bilirubin	
— biliverdin	
— melanogen	

Table 1.2 Differentiation of the causes of the most important changes in the color of the urine

red:	hematuria, hemoglobinuria, myoglobinuria, porphyrinuria, alimentary pigments, rhubarb, senna, beetroot, aminophenazone, aminopyrine, amidopyrine, antipyrine, bromsulphthalein, chrysarubin, diphenylhydantoin, metronidazol, nitrofurantoin, phenacetin, phenothiazine, phenytoin, salazosulfapyridine
yellow-orange:	rhubarb, senna, phenacetin, pyridine and its derivatives, rifampicin, bilirubin
yellow-green:	riboflavin, thymol
brown:	bilirubin (yellow-brown), urobilin (red-brown), hemoglobin, myoglobin, homogentisic acid, melanogen, rhubarb, carotene, aniline derivatives, bromsulphthalein, cascara, chinin, chloroquine, hydroquinone, naphthol, nitrite, nitrofurantoin, imipenem-cilastatin, phenacetin, phenolphthalein, thymol
green:	biliverdin, arbutin, creosot, chlorophyll, flavin, guaiacol, indigo-carmine, methylene blue, santonin, triamterene
blue:	methylene blue, indigo blue
black:	hemoglobinuria, alcaptonuria, melanogen
darkening upon standing:	alcaptonuria, melanogen, serotonin, cascara, chlorpromazine, methyldopa, metronidazole, phenacetin, porphyrin

Centrifugation

Centrifugation is used to separate cellular elements and casts from the bulk of urine fluid. Unless done properly, however, centrifugation may introduce artefacts. Recovery of cellular elements is optimal at 2,500 rpm, but even then recovery is incomplete [4]. Higher forces of acceleration may improve yield, but also cause disruption of the casts or packing of mucus. Lower velocities result in insufficient recovery. The yield is also influenced by the duration of the centrifugation. Five or 10 minutes are usually adopted, *but it is extremely important that one uses always the same time.* The yield is also influenced by the volume of the centrifuged urine. To obtain reproducible results, *the same aliquot of urine* (e.g. 10 ml) *must always be used.*

Spontaneous sedimentation is usually not a valid alternative to centrifugation, but occasionally — specifically in the presence of macrohematuria — spontaneous sedimentation may enable one to observe elements which would be disrupted by centrifugation (e.g., fragile erythrocyte casts or other diagnostically important cellular elements) or masked by densely packed erythrocytes.

Resuspension

After centrifugation, the supernatant is discarded. While many investigators decant the supernatant, we recommend removing a standardized amount of urine, e.g., 9.5 ml per 10 ml, with a pump. This helps to standardize the procedure and increases its reproducibility [5].
The sediment should not be resuspended by shaking the tube, but by gently pulling it into a Pasteur pipette or automatic pipette several times until the entire precipitate is in suspension. If too much precipitate is present, resuspension of only part of the centrifugate is preferred. This procedure avoids packing too many elements onto the slide.

Preparation of slides

An aliquot, preferably a standardized volume of the resuspended urine, is transferred to the slide. We transfer 50 µl of urine with an automatic pipette, since this volume fits under a cover slip of 24×32 mm without spilling [5].

Microscopic examination

One should start by examining at low magnification. First one should examine the edges of the cover slip where casts tend to collect, and then the rest of the specimen. Low magnification is indispensable for rough estimation of the number of casts present. One then proceeds to higher magnification. For every case a sufficient number (10-20) of random microscopic fields should be examined, and even more fields should be examined, if the elements of interest are unevenly distributed, e.g., when casts or cells collect at the edges of the cover slip or when cells are clumped because of mucus.
Once the slide has been prepared it should be examined forthwith, since in the microenvironment between slide and cover slip artefactual changes and even precipitation of crystals are quick to appear, because of heat from the light of the microscope or other causes.
If one wishes to evaluate the sediment, one should aim at recognizing those artefacts due to abnormal urine osmolality and pH. At high osmolality, erythrocytes and leucocytes shrink (figure 1.2). This renders identification of erythrocytes difficult. It also hampers recognition of pathognomonic dysmorphic deformities of erythrocytes. At low osmolality, approximately 360 mOsm/l (or specific gravity 1.009), erythrocytes are lysed [6]. Epithelial cells are not readily lysed, but their morphology is altered and Brownian movement of subcellular elements is seen in the cytoplasm. Casts lyse at high pH. Aggregation of Tamm Horsfall protein, the key constituent of the cast matrix, is pH-dependent and minimal at high pH [7]. The urinary pH may also affect the urinary sediment by its effects on precipitation of crystals, e.g., uric acid at low pH and phosphates at high pH.
In an effort at quantitation, one should report the approximate mean number of elements (or their range) seen per unit area, e.g., 3 erythrocytes/high power field (HPF), or 3-12 erythrocytes/HPF. We prefer such semiquantitative reporting to the common vague classifications as rare, occasional, moderate, severe. The number of casts should be evaluated at low magnification. High power is needed only to identify morphological details of casts. All other elements must be evaluated at higher power.
A report on the urinary sediment should include the following pieces of information (suggested sample of a report form, see figure 1.3):
— osmolality (or specific gravity)

— pH
— protein and hemoglobin (by dip stix)
— erythrocyte number and their morphology
— polymorphonuclear leucocytes (or other leucocyte subtypes)
— epithelial cells. Tubular cells should be differentiated from transitional cells since they have different clinical implications; lumping them under the term "urinary tract cells" is imprecise and should be avoided
— casts (again their morphology should be specified, since the different types have different clinical implications)
— lipids and microorganisms
— in contrast to previous opinion, the amount of mucus or the number of squamous cells are not of clinical relevance. Therefore, these elements are not mentioned in the report.

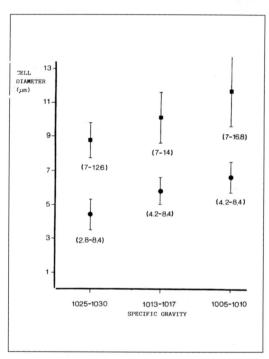

Fig. 1.2 *Changes in cellular size with variations of the specific gravity of the urine. Urine sediments from 5 different patients were evaluated for each range of specific gravity. Forty isomorphic erythrocytes and forty leucocytes were measured for each sediment. Each mean and standard deviation was therefore obtained from 200 measurements.* ●=*erythrocytes.* ■=*leucocytes. The numbers in parentheses indicate the size ranges.*

The microscope

Today examination by phase contrast microscopy is the state of the art for examination of urinary sediment. This technique has largely taken the place of examination of unstained or stained urinary sediments by bright field microscopy.

Bright field microscope

The drawback of the this type of microscope is that it allows only poor visualization of elements with low refractive indexes, e.g., hyaline casts and erythrocytes with low hemoglobin content. Erythrocytes may be confused with yeasts or roundish calcium oxalate crystals, leucocytes may be difficult to differentiate from tubular cells, bacteria may be confused with amorphous material. Although contrast may be increased by reducing the light, e.g., by downward adjustment of the condensor or by closing the diaphragm, the method is clearly not the best.

```
SURNAME.........................NAME.................DATE...............

OSMOLALITY.......................pH..................................
PROTEIN........................HEMOGLOBIN............................
ERYTHROCYTES...................MORPHOLOGY............................
POLYMORPHONUCLEAR LEUCOCYTES.........................................
TUBULAR CELLS.......................................................
TRANSITIONAL CELLS..................................................
CASTS..........................SUBTYPES.............................
....................................................................
LIPIDS..............................................................
BACTERIA.......................YEASTS...............................
OTHER ELEMENTS......................................................
....................................................................
COMMENT.............................................................
....................................................................
....................................................................

                                            SIGNATURE
                                   .....................
```

Fig. 1.3

Fig. 1.4

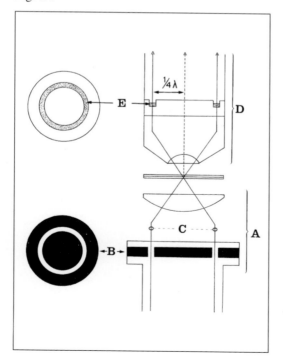

Fig. 1.3 *The urinary sediment report.*

Fig. 1.4 *Schema of the phase contrast microscope.*
A=condenser
B=anular diaphragm
C=hollow cone of light
D=objective
E=phase ring with the layer of translucent silver (dotted gray area)
——▶ *= direct light*
---▶ *= diffracted light*

Phase contrast microscope

Fritz Zernike received the Nobel price for inventing the principle of phase contrast microscopy. A normal microscope can be fitted with phase contrast equipment. The principle is outlined in figure 1.4. The condenser contains an anular diaphragm which transforms the incident light into a hollow cone of light. The objective differs from a conventional one: in its posterior focal plane it contains a circular etched ring, the so-called phase ring, which is covered by a translucent layer of silver. After penetrating the object under study, the light beam is composed of both direct light and diffracted light, the photons of which have interacted with the object. While the direct light passes through the phase ring, the diffracted light passes only through the surrounding thicker areas. This difference in the lengths of the light paths results in a phase difference between the two light beams of one fourth of the wavelength. Such a difference is perceived by the eye as a diminution in light intensity and this underlies the phase contrast effect. The phase contrast microscope is fitted with an ocular which centers the ring of the condenser into the phase ring of the objective. The centering takes only few seconds and is carried out by acting on the two small knobs underneath the condenser. This maneuver has to be done frequently. When changing to an objective with higher power, the anular condenser has to be changed in parallel, since the ring of the anular diaphragm and the ring in the objective must match. For this purpose, modern microscopes have several different anular diaphragms with matching objectives. In phase contrast, unlike in bright field microscopy, the condenser must be adjusted upward and the diaphragm must be kept open if one wishes to obtain maximal light. (For the adjustment of the microscope according to Köhler's principle see Appendix).

If the phase contrast objectives are used with conventional condensers, one can also examine by bright field microscopy with the same microscope. Examination with polarized light is also possible, but the results are not as good as when polarization is performed in connection with a bright field microscope.

A peculiar feature of the phase contrast microscope is the presence of a halo, i.e., a clear zone around dark details and a dark zone around clear details. This phenomenon further enhances contrast, but it may interfere with measurements and reduces the quality of microphotographs. Although the phase contrast microscope is superior for recognition of casts and erythrocyte morphology, one cannot recognize fine details of lymphocytes and eosinophils. For these elements, staining of the urinary sediment is necessary.

It may also be difficult to distinguish blood-derived mononuclear cells from tubular or (small) transitional epithelial cells.

Polarized light

The bright field microscope can be fitted with two polarization filters, one underneath the condenser and the other above the objective. Rotating the lower filter by 90° causes the microscopic field to darken. When an anisotropic object is placed between the two filters, the plane of oscillation of the light beam is shifted by interaction with the anisotropic particle under study and a fraction of light reaches the eye (figure 1.5).

In urine sediments, cholesterol esters and free cholesterol are anisotropic and look like Maltese crosses, i.e., they resemble the cross of the crusader order of Malta (figure 2.56). Many crystals are anisotropic as well. This property distinguishes roundish calcium oxalate crystals (which polarize light) from erythrocytes (which do not), or uric acid crystals (which polarize light) from glass slivers (which do not).

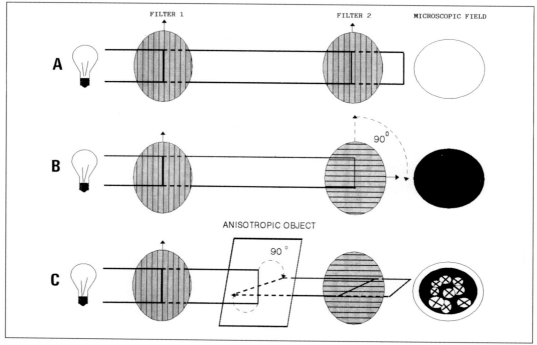

Fig. 1.5 *Principle of the microscope with polarized light.*
A=The two polarization filters are in parallel: the light passes through them both and the microscopic field is visible.
B=Filter 2 is rotated by 90°: the light is absorbed by filter 2 and the microscopic field darkens.
C=An anisotropic object is placed between the two filters: the plane of vibration of the light which has crossed filter 1 is changed and a fraction of the light reaches the eye.

Other techniques

For more sophisticated scientific work, interference contrast microscopy, immunofluorescence microscopy and electron microscopy offer specific advantages.

Interference contrast microscopy provides a three-dimensional image of the object under study [8]. It is expensive, however, and its limited resolution in depth renders it less useful.

Immunofluorescence microscopy has been used to investigate the composition of urinary casts. In some specific conditions, e.g., glomerulonephritis [9] and monoclonal gammopathies [10], immunofluorescence information on protein composition of casts can be useful for diagnostic purposes (see Appendix).
Immunofluorescence utilizing fluorescein-conjugated antibodies to human immunoglobulins is used to demonstrate "antibody coated bacteria". This demonstration permits one to differentiate non-invasive infection from bacterial infection of the urinary tract with invasion of tissues [11].

Scanning electronmicroscopy has helped to further define various types of casts [12] and dysmorphic erythrocytes [13]. It has been claimed that *transmission electronmicroscopy* can be used to identify amyloid fibrils in the urines of patients with amyloidosis [14], but this has been questioned by others [15]. Fibrils may also be found in the urines of patients with myeloma [16]. It has further been reported that by electronmicroscopy one can identify necrotic tubular cells in the urines of patients with acute renal failure [17]. Similarly, myeloid bodies that result from altered phospholipid metabolism of tubular epithelial cells in cases of aminoglycoside nephrotoxicity can be recognized [16] but the technique is certainly not widely applicable.

Stains

While phase contrast microscopy gives superior resolution of details, it is inadequate for identification of the following cellular types:
— *eosinophils* — these are important elements in hypersensitivity reactions
— *lymphocytes* — these are important elements in recognizing rejection crises of the renal allograft,
— *atypical epithelial cells* — these are important to diagnose uroepithelial malignancy (a detailed discussion of this is beyond the scope of this book; for review see reference 18).

Recognition of *eosinophils* requires the use of either the Hansel's stain [19], the panoptic stain of Wright [20], Papanicolaou's stain or May-Grünwald-Giemsa.
For recognition of *lymphocytes*, one may use Wright's stain or — to recognize RNA-rich activated lymphocytes — methylene green pyronin stain [21]. Others have used methylene blue, a supravital stain [22], the Papanicolaou stain [23] or the May-Grünwald-Giemsa stain. Figure 2.25 gives a typical example of lymphocytes in the urine sediment. For technical details about May-Grünwald-Giemsa, see Appendix.
In some particular instances, specific stains may be useful, e.g., oil-red 0 for *lipids* or Prussian blue for *iron* and *hemosiderin*.
Staining with monoclonal antibodies specific for several types of cells of the urinary sediment (granulocytes, lymphocytes, monocytes, glomerular epithelial cells, tubular and urothelial cells) is now possible. With this technique specific cytopathologic profiles have been identified in acute interstitial rejection [24, 25] as well as in rapidly progressive glomerulonephritis, acute interstitial nephritis and acute tubular necrosis [26].
For the historically-minded we mention the obsolete stains of Sternheimer and Malbin [27] and of Prescott and Brody [28].

Quantitation of urinary excretion rates of cells

In principle, there are two different possible ways to quantify the rates of excretion of erythrocytes, leucocytes or epithelial cells. Using counting chambers (or hemocytometers), one may either count the number of cells per unit volume in spontaneously voided urine or else count the cells in 12- or 24-hour urine collections. The former procedure was thoroughly studied by Kesson [29], the latter was introduced by Thomas Addis [30] (see also page 8). The Addis count is no longer popular today: it is laborious, inaccurate and cells or casts may disintegrate in 12-hour urine collections. Moreover, quantifying the cells in counting chambers has some methodological problems. In fact, the Fuchs Rosenthal chamber, for example, gives variable results [31]. Some of the reasons for variability are listed in table 1.3.

Table 1.3 Sources of errors observed with the cell counting chambers
(adapted from reference 31)

ERRORS IN CALIBRATION AND FILLING
Inaccuracies of the quadratic pattern of the chamber
Variations of the depth of the chamber
Non-planar coverslip
Poor positioning of the coverslip
ERRORS INHERENT IN THE URINE
Tendency of cells to clump
Tendency of cells to move towards the lines of the grid
Entrapping of elements by mucus

Recommended procedures

Table 1.4 summarizes the procedures used in our laboratory for routine examination of urinary sediment.

Table 1.4 Recommended procedures for the preparation and analysis of the urinary
sediments, as used in our laboratory

Collection of midstream urine in clean plastic containers with covers
Prompt sample handling and analysis
Standardized centrifugation i.e., 2,000 rpm for 10 minutes, 10 ml aliquot of urine (centrifugation is not performed in case of gross hematuria or of strong turbidity of urine)
Removal of a fixed volume of supernatant urine i.e., 9.5 ml, by suction
Gentle but thorough resuspension of the precipitate in the remaining 0.5 ml of urine with an automatic pipette
Transfer of a fixed volume of resuspended urine, i.e., 50 µl, to a grease-free slide by an automatic pipette
Covering of the sample with a coverslip 24×32 mm
Urinary sediment scan by phase contrast microscope equipped with two objectives (16X and 40X) and a 10X binocular (Stains are used only for the search of eosinophils. Polarized light is used to identify doubtful lipids and crystals).
Elements of the urinary sediment semiquantified as ranges per low (casts) or high power field (all the other elements). At least 20 microscopic fields are examined

References

[1] BURTON J.R., ROWE J.W., HILL R.N.: *Quantitation of casts in urine sediment.* Ann. Intern. Med., 83: 518-9 (letter), 1975.

[2] HOCKBERGER R.S., SCHWARTZ B., CONNOR J.: *Hematuria induced by urethral catheterization.* Ann. Emerg. Med., 16: 550-2, 1987.

[3] ROTH S., RENNER E., RATHERT P.: *Microscopic hematuria: advances in identification of glomerular dysmorphic erythrocytes.* J. Urol., 146: 680-4, 1991.

[4] GADEHOLT H.: *Quantitative estimation of urinary sediment, with special regard to sources of error.* Brit. Med. J., 1: 1547-9, 1964.

[5] FOGAZZI G.B., PASSERINI P., BAZZI M., et al.: *Use of high power field in the evaluation of formed elements of urine.* J. Nephrol., 2: 107-12, 1989.

[6] GADEHOLT H.: *Persistence of blood cells in urine.* Acta Med. Scand., 183: 49-54, 1968.

[7] McQUEEN E.G., ENGEL G.B.: *Factors determining the aggregation of urinary mucoprotein.* J. Clin. Pathol., 19: 392-6, 1966.

[8] HABER M.H.: *Interference contrast microscopy for identification of urinary sediments.* Am. J. Clin. Pathol., 57: 316-9, 1972.

[9] FAIRLEY J.K., OWEN J.E., BIRCH D.F.: *Protein composition of urinary casts from healthy subjects and patients with glomerulonephritis.* Brit. Med. J., 287: 1838-40, 1983.

[10] FOGAZZI G.B., POZZI C., PASSERINI P., et al.: *Utility of immunofluorescence of urine sediment for identifying patients with renal disease due to monoclonal gammopathies.* Am. J. Kidney Dis., 17: 211-7, 1991.

[11] THOMAS V., SHELOKOV A., FORLAND M.: *Antibody-coated bacteria in the urine and the site of urinary-tract infection.* New Engl. J. Med., 290: 588-90, 1974.

[12] HABER M.H., LINDNER L.E.: *The surface ultrastructure of urinary casts.* Am. J. Clin. Pathol., 68: 547-52, 1977.

[13] FASSET R.G., HORGAN B., GOVE D., et al.: *Scanning electron microscopy of glomerular and non glomerular red blood cells.* Clin. Nephrol., 20: 11-6, 1983.

[14] DEROSENA R., KOSS M.N., PIRANI C.L.: *Demonstration of amyloid fibrils in urinary sediment.* New Engl. J. Med., 293: 1131-3, 1975.

[15] SHIRAMA T., SKINNER M., COHEN A.S., et al.: *Uncertain value of urinary sediments in the diagnosis of amyloidosis.* New Engl. J. Med., 297: 821-3, 1977.

[16] MANDAL A.K.: *Assessment of urinary sediment by electron microscopy. Application in renal disease.* New York: Plenum, 186, 1987.

[17] MANDAL A.K., SKLAR A.H., HUDSON J.B.: *Transmission electron microscopy of urinary sediment in human acute renal failure.* Kidney Intern., 28: 58-63, 1985.

[18] SCHUMANN G.B., WEISSS M.A.: *Atlas of renal and urinary tract cytology and its histopathologic bases.* Philadelphia: Lippincott, 237-87, 1981.

[19] NOLAN C.R. III, ANGER M.S., KELLEHER S.P.: *Eosinophiluria — A new method of detection and definition of the clinical spectrum.* New Engl. J. Med., 315: 1516-8, 1986.

[20] CORWIN H.L., HABER M.H.: *The clinical significance of eosinophiluria.* Am. J. Clin. Pathol., 88: 520-2, 1987.

[21] HRUSHESKY W., SAMPSON D., MURPHY G.P.: *Lymphocyturia in human renal allograft rejection.* Arch. Surg., 105: 424-6, 1972.

[22] KRISHNA G.G., FELLER S.K.: *Lymphocyturia: an important diagnostic and prognostic marker in renal allograft rejection.* Am. J. Nephrol., 2: 185-8, 1982.

[23] SCHUMANN G.B., BURLESON R.L., HENRY J.B., et al.: *Urinary cytodiagnosis of acute renal allograft rejection using the cytocentrifuge.* Am. J. Clin. Pathol., 67: 134-40, 1977.

[24] DOOPER I.M.M., BOGMAN M.J.J.T., HOIRSMA A.J., et al.: *Immunocytology of urinary sediments as a method of differentiating acute rejection from other causes of declining renal graft function.* Transplantation 52: 266-71, 1991.

[25] SEGASOTHY M., BIRCH D.F., FAIRLEY K.F., et al.: *Urine cytologic profile in renal allograft recipients determined by monoclonal antibodies.* Transplantation, 47: 482-7, 1989.

[26] SEGASOTHY M., FAIRLEY K.F., BIRCH D.F., et al.: *Immunoperoxidase identification of nucleated cells in urine in glomerular and acute tubular disorders.* Clin. Nephrol., 31: 281-91, 1989.

[27] STERNHEIMER R., MALBIN B.: *Clinical recognition of pyelonephritis, with a new stain for urinary sediments.* Am. J. Med., 11: 312-23, 1951.

[28] PRESCOTT L.F., BRODIE D.E.: *A simple differential stain for urinary sediment.* Lancet, 2: 940, 1964.

[29] KESSOM A.M., TALBOTT J.M., GYORY A.Z.: *Microscopic examination of urine.* Lancet, 2: 809-12, 1978.

[30] ADDIS T.: *A clinical classification of Bright's disease.* JAMA, 85: 163-7, 1925.

[31] GADEHOLT H.: *Counting of cells in urine. The variability of haemocytometer counts.* Acta Med. Scand., 183: 9-16, 1968.

Chapter 2

The formed elements of the urinary sediment

Erythrocytes

Erythrocytes are one of several types of cells which are found in the urinary sediments (table 2.1). Urinary erythrocytes are of variable diameter, index of refractivity and morphology. The mean diameter is about 6 μm (table 2.1 bis), but it is influenced by changes in osmolality, increasing as osmolality decreases (figure 1.2). It is important to remember that at osmolalities below 360 mOsm/l (which is to say specific gravity less than 1.009) the erythrocytes lyse. The refractivity index varies according to the hemoglobin content of the cell. When this is very low, the erythrocyte is difficult to recognize, a thin cell membrane being the only identifiable structure (so called "ghost cell") (figure 2.9). Morphology ranges from perfectly round cells to elements of radically altered shape. This was already noted several decades ago (see page 8), but only recently has it been recognized that there is relationship between some morphological changes of the urinary erythrocytes and the site of the bleeding in the urinary tract. In 1982 Fairley and Birch [1] first reported that the hematuria of glomerular origin is characterized by excretion of erythrocytes with distorted shape (so-called " *dysmorphic erythrocytes*"), in contrast with excretion of erythrocytes with normal shape in hematuria of non-glomerular origin (so-called *"isomorphic erythrocytes"*). According to Fasset et al. [2] hematuria should be classified as "glomerular" if at least 80% of the erythrocytes are dysmorphic and "non-glomerular" if isomorphic, and "mixed" if the two types of cells are of roughly equal percentage. Using these criteria, the utility of the method has been proved by several investigators, who found a sensitivity of about 95% or more for both glomerular and non glomerular types of hematuria [1-5].

If the original classification of urinary erythrocytes is adhered to, cells hard to interpret are occasionally encountered and subjective evaluation may be a major problem in some instances. This may account for the low interobserver reproducibility found in one study [6]. Recent studies, in an attempt to eliminate subjective evaluations have critically analyzed the various erythrocyte morphologies seen in both glomerular and non glomerular bleeding [7, 8], and have proposed new classifications, which include *several types of both dysmorphic* (figures 2.1-2.8) *and isomorphic erythrocytes* (figures 2.9-2.15). A recent breakthrough has been identification of the *acanthocyte* as a reliable marker of glomerular disease when it represents more than 5% of all erythrocytes (specificity 98%, sensitivity 52%) [9]. Acanthocytes are ringformed erythrocytes with vesicle shaped or club-like protrusions, as illustrated in figures 2.16-2.18.

Although excretion of dysmorphic erythrocytes is tantamount to the presence of glomerular disease, exceptions have been encountered. Van Iseghem et al. [10] observed a patient with acute postinfectious glomerulonephritis and gross hematuria whose urinary erythrocytes became increasingly dysmorphic as the hematuria cleared, while in our experience, dysmorphic erythrocytes gradually disappear when patients go into renal failure [11]. Excretion of dysmorphic erythrocytes also depends on the degree of diuresis, since the percentage of dysmorphic erythrocytes decreases after water administration or treatment with furosemide [12].Some patients with necrotizing glomerulonephritis have been found to have isomorphic erythrocytes [13] and this has been confirmed by our own observation [14]. There is no denying, however, that *examination of the urine for dysmorphic erythrocytes is the single most important step in making the diagnosis of glomerulonephritis.*

The cause of the characteristic change in erythrocyte morphology is not clear. Erythrocytes may undergo changes in shape as they pass through gaps in the glomerular basement membrane, as documented by electronmicroscopy [15]. It has become clear, however, that dysmorphic changes can also be induced by osmotic forces when the erythrocytes pass through the tubule. Erythrocytes are sensitized to osmotic shock and the attendant morphological alterations when the plasma membrane has been exposed to enzymatic attack or to the action of detergents. Schramek et al [16] found that a prerequisite for obtaining red cell dysmorphism in vitro is the serial incubation of normal serum erythrocytes in solutions corresponding to those of different parts of the tubular system. In the experiment, however, erythrocytes became dysmorphic only when they were also incubated in a solution containing a hemolytic substance, obtained by a red cell lysate. This leads to the proposal that *in vivo* some of the erythrocytes entering the tubular system may release their cytoplasmic contents and thus catalyze the development of dysmorphic changes.

Table 2.1 The cells of the urinary sediment

	TYPE	SUBTYPE
BLOOD-DERIVED CELLS	ERYTHROCYTES	Isomorphic Dysmorphic Acanthocytes
	LEUCOCYTES	Neutrophils Eosinophils* Lymphocytes*
	HISTIOCYTES**	—
EPITHELIAL CELLS	TUBULAR	Round, columnar oval, polygonal
	TRANSITIONAL	from deep layers from superficial layers of uroepithelium
	SQUAMOUS	—

* = identifiable only after staining (see text, pages 19 and 140).
** = further studies are necessary to confirm the real presence of these cells.

Table 2.1 bis Diameter (μm) of cells found in the urinary sediment

	Number of patients	Number of Cells	Diameter Cell#	Nucleus#
Erythrocytes	15	600	5.6±1.2	—
Neutrophils	15	600	10.3±3.4	—
Tubular cells	5	200	13.2±2.3	7.7±1.1
Transitional cells*	5	200	31.1±9.0	10.1±1.7
Squamous cells	5	200	55.4±9.1	9.4±2.0

Mean±SD.   * superficial layers

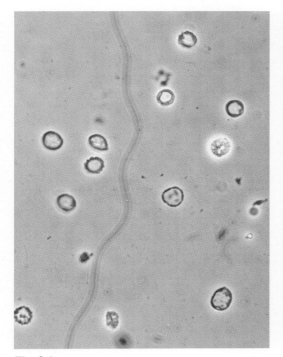

Fig. 2.1

Fig. 2.3

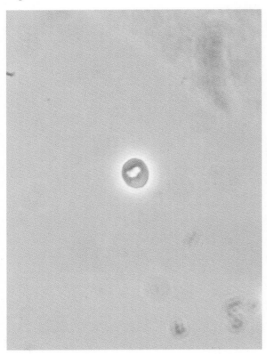

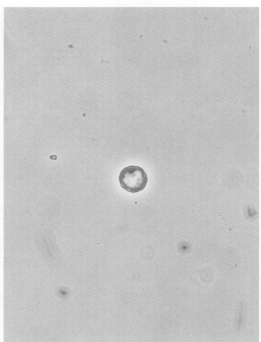

Fig. 2.2

Fig. 2.1 *Ring-shaped dysmorphic erythrocytes (phase contrast, X640).*

Fig. 2.2 *Ring-shaped dysmorphic erythrocyte with irregular cellular membrane (phase contrast, X640).*

Fig. 2.3 *Ring-shaped dysmorphic erythrocyte with global swelling of the cellular membrane (phase contrast, X640).*

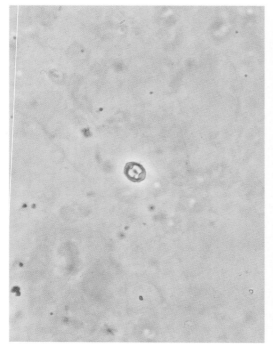

Fig. 2.4

Fig. 2.5`

Fig. 2.6

Fig. 2.7

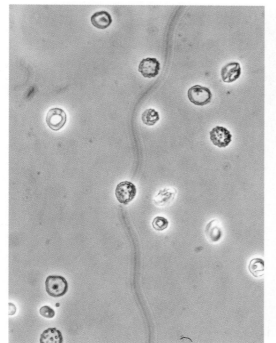

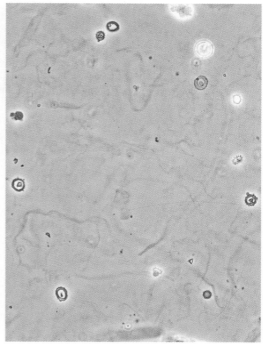

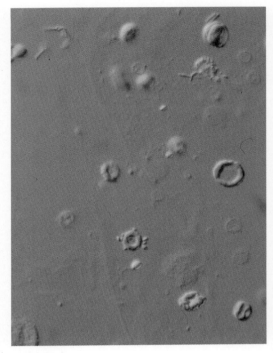

Fig. 2.8

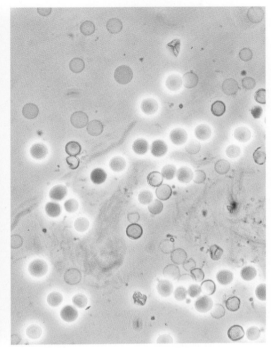

Fig. 2.9

Fig. 2.10

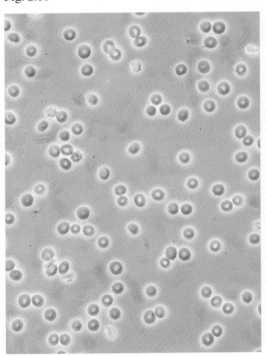

Fig. 2.4 *Ring-shaped dysmorphic erythrocyte with a central protrusion (phase contrast, X640).*

Fig. 2.5 *Ring-shaped erythrocytes with and without central protrusions seen under the interference contrast microscope (X800).*

Fig. 2.6 *Different types of ring-shaped dysmorphic erythrocytes (phase contrast, X640).*

Fig. 2.7 *Several types of dysmorphic erythrocytes in the same sediment (phase contrast, X640).*

Fig. 2.8 *Several types of dysmorphic erythrocytes seen under the interference contrast microscope (X800).*

Fig. 2.9 *Isomorphic erythrocytes looking like perfect spheres. Many of these cells, devoid of hemoglobin look like empty circles (so-called ghost erythrocytes) (phase contrast, X640).*

Fig. 2.10 *Isomorphic erythrocytes with a central pale zone (phase contrast, X400).*

G.B. Fogazzi, P. Passerini, C. Ponticelli, E. Ritz

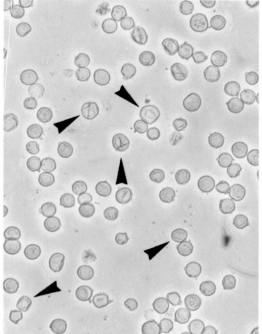

Fig. 2.11

Fig. 2.13

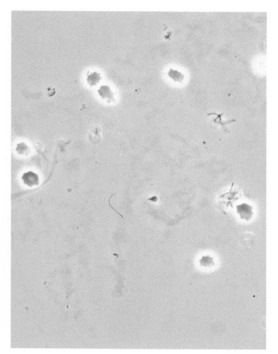

Fig. 2.12

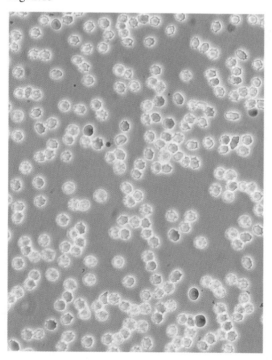

Fig. 2.11 *"Doughnut" isomorphic erythrocytes (arrows) intermingled with many spherocytes (phase contrast, X640).*

Fig. 2.12 *Isomorphic erythrocytes with irregular contours but still with well-preserved cellular membranes (phase contrast, X400).*

Fig. 2.13 *Isomorphic crenated erythrocytes, characterized by regular cytoplasmic projections (phase contrast, X400).*

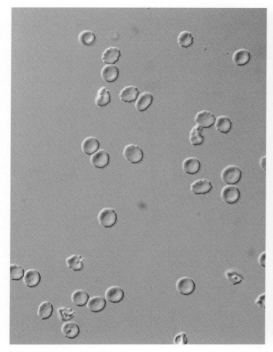

Fig. 2.14

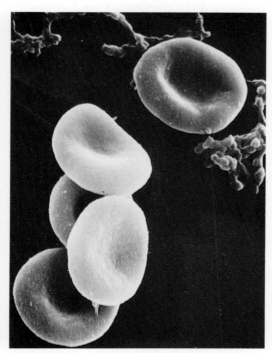

Fig. 2.15

Fig. 2.16

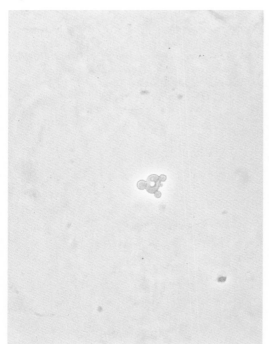

Fig. 2.14 *Isomorphic erythrocytes (biconcave disks and cells with slight irregularities of the contours) seen under the interference contrast microscope (X500).*

Fig. 2.15 *Biconcave isomorphic erythrocytes seen in the scanning electron microscope (X5,000) (courtesy of Doctor Eveline Wandel, Mainz. Reproduced from Stein G., Ritz E.: Diagnostik und Differentialdiagnostik der Nierenerkrankungen. Jena: Gustav Fischer Verlag, 1991. Used with permission).*

Fig. 2.16 *Acanthocyte (phase contrast, X640).*

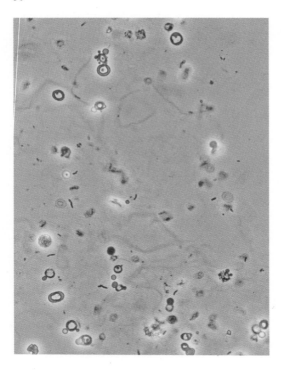

Fig. 2.17 *Glomerular hematuria containing many acanthocytes (patient with acute lupus nephritis) (phase contrast, X500).*

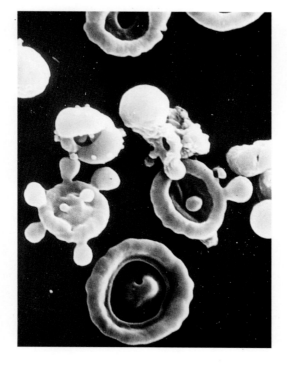

Fig. 2.18 *Acanthocytes and other dysmorphic erythrocytes as seen with the scanning electron microscope (X5,000) (courtesy of Doctor Eveline Wandel, Mainz. Reproduced from Stein G., Ritz E.: Diagnostik und Differentialdiagnostik der Nierenerkrankungen. Jena: Gustav Fischer Verlag, 1991. Used with permission).*

Leucocytes

Polymorphonuclear neutrophils are the type of leucocyte most frequently seen in the urinary sediment. Typically they appear as *round granular cells* (figure 2.19) with a mean diameter of about 10 µm (table 2.1 bis). The diameter may greatly vary, however, as a function of osmolality (figure 1.2). Osmolality influences leucocyte morphology too. In fact, in concentrated urine, the cytoplasmic organelles are packed and identification of the nucleus may be difficult. In contrast, in dilute urine the cytoplasmic granules are scattered and undergo Brownian movement. The lobulated nucleus is then also clearly visible (figure 2.20). Occasionally, neutrophils have multiple small blebs (figure 2.21) or are elongated in shape (figure 2.22). Interpretation of these changes is not easy. Frequently neutrophils degenerate so that the distinction between nucleus and cytoplasm is lost and the cell shape is drastically altered (figure 2.21). Neutrophils can be also in clumps (figure 2.23), which are more frequently found in urinary tract infections. Usually neutrophils can be identified easily. However, in concentrated urine it may be difficult to differentiate them from the small tubular cells or from other blood-derived cells. Differentiation may be helped by addition of a few drops of acetic acid, after which the nuclear membranes become more clearly visible. Urinary tract infections are the most frequent cause of neutrophiluria, but this is not specific for bacterial infection. It may also be observed in conditions as diverse as proliferative glomerulonephritis, polycystic kidney disease and analgesic nephropathy. Neutrophiluria can also be observed in acute appendicitis or acute adnexitis, i.e., with inflammation of organs next to the urinary tract. Neutrophils in the urine may also reflect contamination by genital secretions. The presence of other cells, e.g., vaginal epithelial cells helps to differentiate contamination from true leucocyturia.

Eosinophils may also be present. They can definitely be identified only by using the staining procedures of Papanicolaou, Wright or Hansel (see page 19). They have a bilobar nucleus and well defined eosinophilic granules. These occupy the entire cytoplasm (figure 2.24). Eosinophils may be observed in urinary tract infections, when they usually comprise less than 5% of total leucocytes. A higher percentage of eosinophils is found in acute interstitial nephritis secondary to drug allergy [17] or in cholesterol embolism of the kidney [18].

Lymphocytes appear as small round cells with a large nucleus and a thin pale cytoplasmic rim (figure 2.25). They can only be identified reliably in stained preparations (see page 19). Lymphocytes are observed in the urine of transplant patients during acute cellular rejection episodes and may have a role in its diagnosis (see page 128). This has been demonstrated by several studies, sensitivity being about 90% [19, 20]. Of interest, in about half of the cases the appearance of lymphocyturia preceded the clinical signs of rejection.

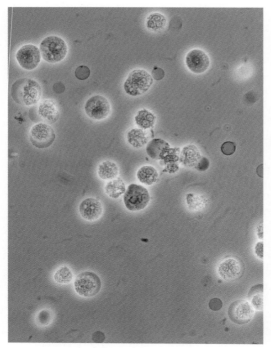

Fig. 2.19

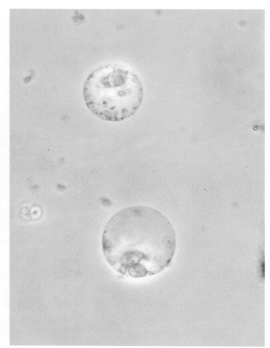

Fig. 2.20

Fig. 2.21

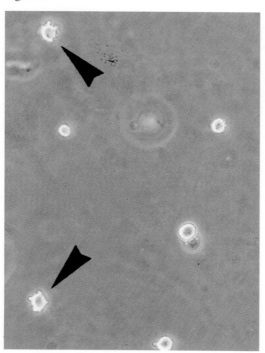

Fig. 2.19 *Polymorphonuclear leucocytes. Phase contrast microscopy clearly shows the granular cytoplasm and the segmented nucleus (X500).*

Fig. 2.20 *Swollen polymorphonuclear leucocytes, apparently with few cytoplasmic organelles, as they appear in urine with low osmolality (phase contrast, X640).*

Fig. 2.21 *Polymorphonuclear leucocytes with cytoplasmic blebs (arrows) (phase contrast, X400).*

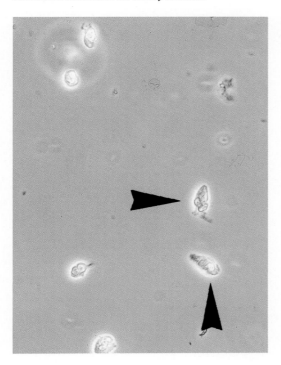

Fig. 2.22 *Elongated polymorphonuclear leuco-cytes (arrows) (phase contrast, X400).*

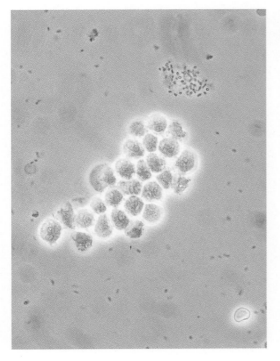

Fig. 2.23 *A small clump of polymorphonuclear leucocytes plus bacteria, a typical finding in urinary tract infections (phase contrast, X400).*

G.B. Fogazzi, P. Passerini, C. Ponticelli, E. Ritz

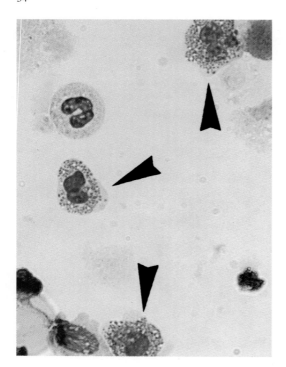

Fig. 2.24 *Eosinophils with their abundant gran-ules (arrows) (May-Grünwald-Giemsa, X1,000).*

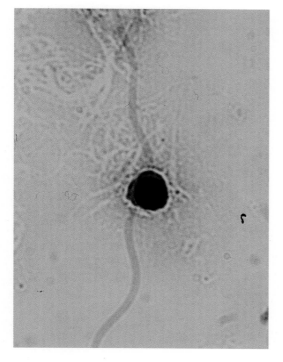

Fig. 2.25 *Lymphocyte (May-Grünwald-Giemsa, X1,000).*

Histiocytes

Histiocytes in the urinary sediment were reported by *Rivas Manga and Cifuentes Delatte* in 1973 [21]. The histiocytes were described as cells with variable morphology and diameters ranging from 15 to 30 μm. In phase contrast microscopy, histiocytes appear as flat polygonal cells with gray granular cytoplasm or as elongated cells with pseudopods of variable length and shape (figures 2.26 and 2.27). They are usually associated with leucocytes and are found in urinary tract infections, interstitial nephritis, urolithiasis, prostatitis and in the healing phases following prostatectomy. If the cells give a positive Gomori stain, which is specific for acid phosphatase, and have the characteristic ultrastructural features, they are probably true histiocytes.

With the phase contrast microscope we have observed similar cells in the urinary sediment. They were always accompanied by polymorphonuclear leucocytes. We have seen, however, that within seconds to minutes leucocytes may be transformed into polygonal gray cells resembling histiocytes. This observation suggests that cells with the above morphology may, at least occasionally, be degenerated leucocytes rather than histiocytes. Further studies are necessary to elucidate the real presence of these cells in the urine and their diagnostic importance.

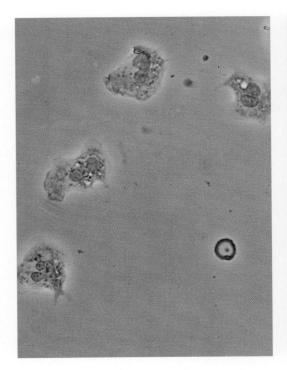

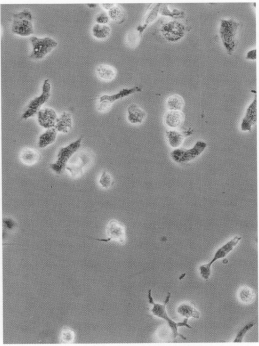

Fig. 2.26 *Histiocytes with gray and granular cytoplasm (phase contrast, X500).*

Fig. 2.27 *Tuberous and dendritic histiocytes mixed with polymorphonuclear cells (phase contrast, X400).*

Renal tubular cells

The different segments of the renal tubules are composed of several types of cells. They differ in shape (flat vs columnar), location of the nucleus (basal vs central), cytoplasmic organelles (scarce vs abundant) and membranes (extensive vs scarce infolding of basolateral membrane and/or interdigitation; cells with or without brush border). The enormous spectrum of morphological appearance of tubular epithelial cells is shown in figures 2.28-2.31. Under appropriate clinical conditions all these subtypes of tubular cells may appear in the urine, but only a few of them can be identified in the sediment by microscopy. As a consequence, investigators usually categorize cells only as of "tubular" origin. The most frequently found "tubular" cells have a mean diameter of about 13 μm (table 2.1 bis). They are round to oval, with a large central or eccentric nucleus, containing one or two nucleoli and a cytoplasm with well defined organelles (figure 2.32). Other cells are rectangular or polygonal with a central nucleus (figures 2.33 and 2.34) or of tall columnar shape, with a nucleus in the basal position and with prominent nucleoli (figure 2.35). Tubular cells are mostly single, but they can also be seen in small clumps (figure 2.36); occasionally they are embedded in casts. This is especially true for the round subtype (figure 2.88, 2.89).

It can be difficult to differentiate the round or ovoid tubular cells from mononuclear blood cells, e.g. monocytes or basophils. Moreover, tubular cells are easily confounded with small ovoid cells from the deep (germinative) layers of the uroepithelium (figure 2.37). The most useful clue to differentiate the two cell types is the context in which they are seen: tubular cells are usually accompanied by elements indicative of parenchymal renal disease, such as casts, dysmorphic erythrocytes or lipids. Transitional cells are more commonly associated with isomorphic erythrocytes, leucocytes, bacteria or crystals.

Tubular cells may be found not only in disorders that primarily involve the tubules, e.g., acute tubular necrosis, acute upper urinary tract infection and acute allograft rejection, but also in glomerular diseases with a nephritic or nephrotic syndrome. It is thought that tubular cells are sloughed off when high protein concentrations in the filtrate exceed the reabsorptive capacity of tubular cells, leading to cell degeneration. Other causes for tubular cell sloughing are viral infections or exposure to nephrotoxic drugs.

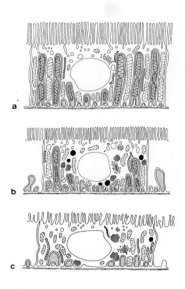

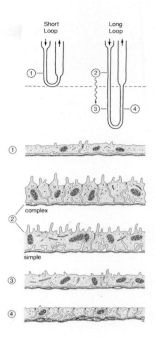

Fig. 2.28

Fig. 2.30

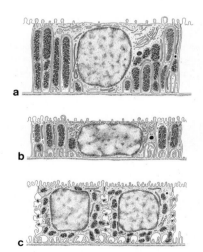

Fig. 2.29

Fig. 2.28 *Ultrastructure of cells of proximal tubule. a) Cell of S1 segment, with very extensive cell interdigitation and high and dense brush border. b) Cell of S2 segment, with reduced interdigitation and less dense brush border. c) Cell of S3 segment, the cellular interdigitation and brush border of which is drastically reduced. (*)*

Fig. 2.29 *Ultrastructure of cells of Henle's loop. 1) Cells of thin limb of short loops. 2) Cells of thin limb of long loops (the complex type is found, for instance, in rat and mouse; the simple type is found, for instance, in rabbit and guinea pig). 3) Cells of the lower part of the descending thin limb of long loops. 4) Cells of ascending thin limb. (*)*

Fig. 2.30 *Ultrastructure of cells of distal straight tubule including macula densa. a) Medullary part. b) Cortical part. c) Macula densa. (*)*

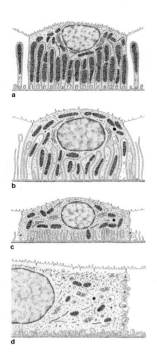

Fig. 2.31

Fig. 2.33

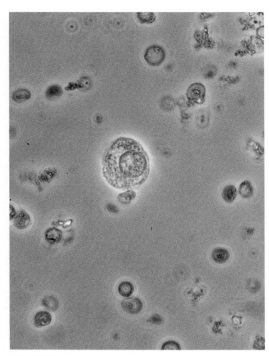

Fig. 2.32

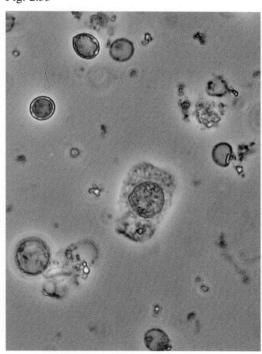

Fig. 2.31 *Ultrastructure of cells of distal convoluted tubule (a), connecting tubule (b), collecting duct (principal cell) (c), and inner medullary collecting duct (d). (*)*

* Courtesy of Doctors Kriz W. and Kaissling B., Heidelberg. Reproduced from: "The Kidney: Physiology and Pathophysiology, Second Edition. Seldin D.W. and Giebisch G. editors. New York: Raven Press, 1992. (Used with permission).

Fig. 2.32 *Ovoid renal tubular cell with central nucleus (phase contrast, X500).*

Fig. 2.33 *Rectangular renal tubular cell (phase contrast, X640).*

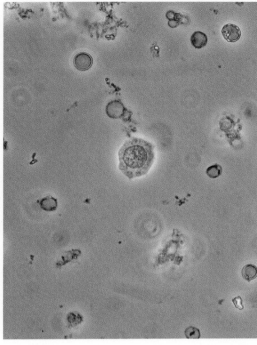

Fig. 2.34

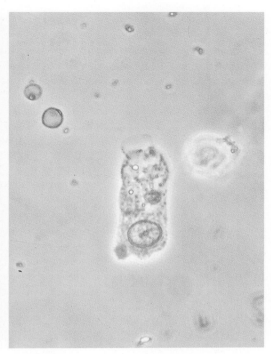

Fig. 2.35

Fig. 2.36

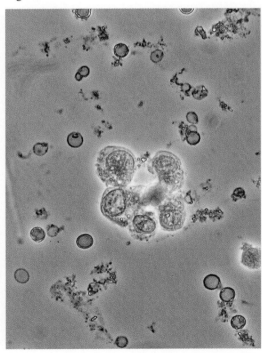

Fig. 2.34 *Polygonal renal tubular cell (phase contrast, X500).*

Fig. 2.35 *Columnar renal tubular cell, with a peripheral nucleus and a very evident nucleolus (phase contrast, X800).*

Fig. 2.36 *Clump of ovoid renal tubular cells (phase contrast, X500).*

Transitional cells (uroepithelium)

The uroepithelium lines the urinary tract from the calyces to the bladder in women, and to the proximal urethra in men. It is a multilayered epithelium, with two main types of cells: the cells of the deep layers and the cells of the superficial layers. Both types of cells can be found in the urinary sediments.

Transitional cells of the *deeper layers* of the uroepithelium are smaller and more heterogeneous than the superficial cells. Besides small ovoid cells, cells with more exotic shapes, e.g. "tailed", "club", and "hammer" cells are encountered.

Small ovoid cells have a large central nucleus and a thin cytoplasmic rim, resembling the round ovoid cells of the renal tubules (figures 2.37 and 2.38). Tailed and club cells have large peripheral nuclei and prominent nucleoli as well as dense granular cytoplasm (figures 2.39 and 2.40). Hammer cells may be binucleated (figure 2.41). The presence of these cells in the urinary sediments indicates that the deep layers of the uroepithelium are damaged, which, in our experience, happens only for severe diseases such as malignancies or stones.

The cells of the *superficial layers* of the urothelium are larger than those of the deep layers, their size ranging from 18 to 39 μm with a mean of about 30 μm (table 2.1 bis). They are round to oval, with round or oval nuclei located in central or only slightly eccentric position. Occasionally binucleated cells are seen. The cytoplasmic granules are usually scarce around the nucleus and abundant in the periphery, resulting in a perinuclear halo (figures 2.42-2.45). These cells are easily identified and frequently seen in urinary sediments, since even mild injury to the uroepithelium causes their exfoliation. In our experience, these cells are a frequent finding in lower urinary tract infections.

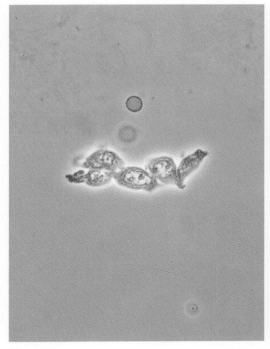

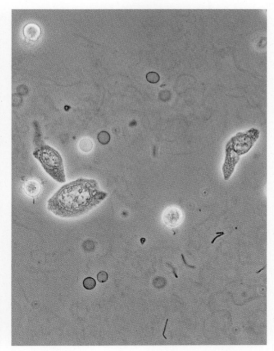

Fig. 2.37

Fig. 2.38

Fig. 2.39

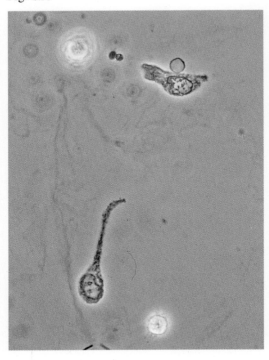

Fig. 2.37 *Small ovoid cells of the deep urothelium (phase contrast, X400).*

Fig. 2.38 *Club and ovoid cells of the deep urothelium (phase contrast, X400).*

Fig. 2.39 *Tailed and ovoid cells of the deep urothelium (phase contrast, X400).*

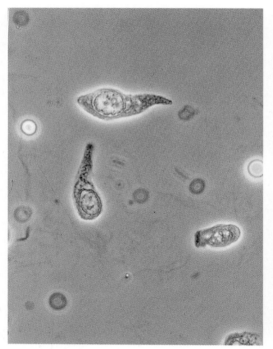

Fig. 2.40

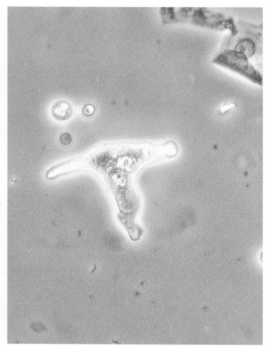

Fig. 2.41

Fig. 2.42

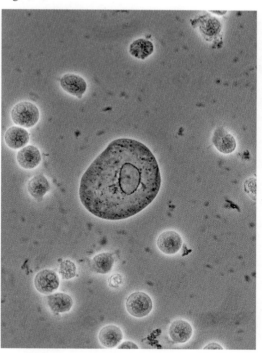

Fig. 2.40 *Ovoid, tailed and club cells of the deep urothelium (phase contrast, X400).*

Fig. 2.41 *Hammer-shaped cell of the deep urothelium containing two nuclei (phase contrast, X320).*

Fig. 2.42 *Large ovoid cell of the superficial urothelium and polymorphonuclear leucocytes. Note the different size of the two types of cells (phase contrast, X400).*

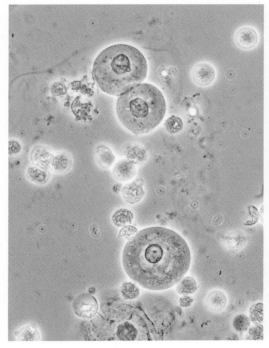

Fig. 2.43

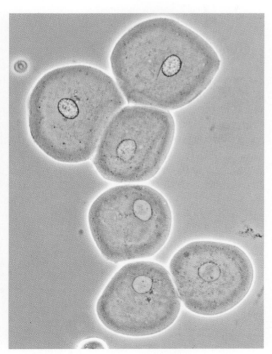

Fig. 2.44

Fig. 2.45

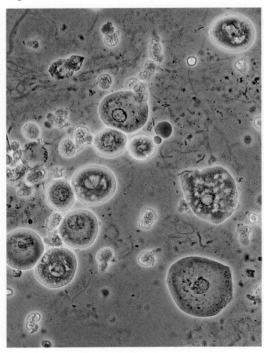

Fig. 2.43 *Round cells of the superficial urothelium (phase contrast, X400).*

Fig. 2.44 *Clump of large cells of the superficial urothelium (phase contrast, X400).*

Fig. 2.45 *Cells of the superficial urothelium with different diameters (phase contrast, X400).*

Squamous cells

Squamous cells are contaminants rather than elements of diagnostic significance. Squamous cells are the largest cells in the urinary sediment. Their mean diameter is about 55 μm, ranging from 35 to 77 (table 2.1 bis). These cells are quadrangular to polygonal in shape, and have a broad cytoplasm containing few granules and a small central nucleus (figure 2.46). Frequently, squamous cells are folded or are aggregated in clumps (figure 2.47). Occasionally, bacteria are attached to their cytoplasm (figure 2.48) reflecting colonization by bacteria, a process which is thought to be an indispensable step in the genesis of urinary tract infection. After cell degeneration, isolated free nuclei may be seen in the sediment (figure 2.49).

Squamous cells are constantly shed from the urethra and vagina and are therefore often present in the urinary sediment, usually in small numbers. However, in the presence of vaginal discharge and infection squamous cells can be so abundant that proper analysis of the urinary sediment is impeded. Vaginal cells (and, in parallel, cells of the posterior urethra of the woman) undergo cyclical changes during the menstrual cycle; after staining estrogenic and luteal phases can be clearly distinguished, as shown in figure 2.50. If many squamous cells are present but there are no leucocytes, such cells may originate from the posterior urethra. If squamous cells are accompanied by numerous leucocytes, contamination by vaginal discharge must be suspected. The diagnosis of urinary tract infection must not be made unless vaginal contamination is excluded by strict adherence to midstream collection techniques in repeat examinations.

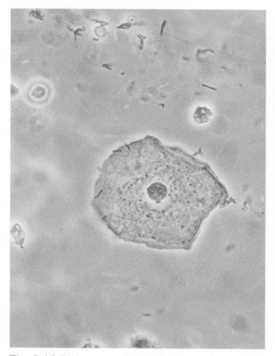

Fig. 2.46 *Squamous cell (with a few rods attached to the cytoplasm) (phase contrast, X320).*

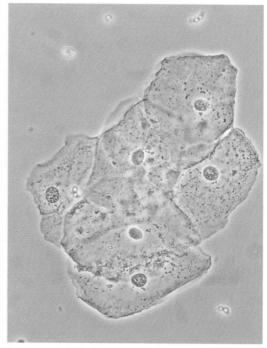

Fig. 2.47 *Clump of squamous cells (phase contrast, X400).*

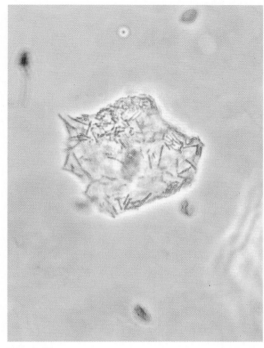

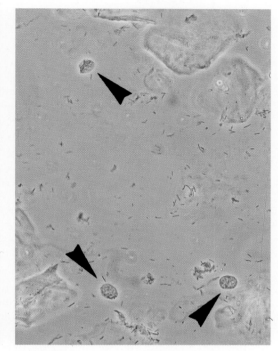

Fig. 2.48

Fig. 2.49

Fig. 2.50

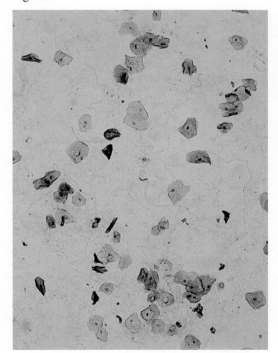

Fig. 2.48 *Many rods adhering to the cytoplasm of a squamous cell (phase contrast, X500).*

Fig. 2.49 *Free nuclei of disrupted squamous cells (arrows), a frequent finding in sediments containing large amounts of these cells (phase contrast, X400).*

Fig. 2.50 *Squamous azurophilic and eosinophilic cells in a woman's urine. The different stain properties are due to different degrees of cell maturation (Uristain, X100).*

Lipids

Lipids may be present in the urinary sediment as free lipid droplets, oval fat bodies, fatty casts and cholesterol crystals.

Free lipid droplets appear as translucent round particles without central structure. They are pale green in bright field microscopy and bright yellow in phase contrast microscopy. They are usually small but occasionally they may be larger than erythrocytes (figure 2.51).

Oval fat bodies are cells of oval, round or irregular shape, laden with aggregated lipid globules. The globules are of variable size and may even confer polycyclic edges to the oval fat bodies (figures 2.52 and 2.53). Elongated spicules or plates with straight margins resembling free cholesterol crystals may protrude from the oval fat bodies (figure 2.54). Cellular structures can still be visible between loosely packed lipid droplets (figure 2.55). The size of oval fat bodies is variable.

Lipid particles, free or within the oval fat bodies, can usually be identified without difficulty. However, larger fat globules may be confused with erythrocytes, yeasts or round calcium oxalate crystals. If scarce and tiny, on the other hand, they may be overlooked. Occasionally the features of oval fat bodies are atypical. It is welcome therefore that lipids can be identified positively in polarized light, which identifies lipids by the appearance of "Maltese crosses" (figure 2.56). False positive birefringence may be due to starch crystals, a frequent contaminant of the urinary sediment (see page 100). Starch crystals are usually larger and the "cross" is asymmetrical (figure 2.183). Only lipids containing cholesterol esters and free cholesterol crystals will show up as "Maltese crosses" under polarized light. Neutral fat, free fatty acids and phospholipids are isotropic and do not show the "Maltese cross" phenomenon. Lipids can also be identified by stains, e.g., Oil Red 0 or Sudan III. These stains are too time consuming for routine purposes, however.

Lipid droplets and oval fat bodies are typical of, but not specific for, nephrotic syndrome. They may also be found in patients with non-nephrotic proteinuria and even in some patients without glomerular disease [22]. Lipid bodies have also been observed in the urine of patients with polycystic kidney disease with low grade proteinuria [23]; in these patients the lipid droplets were found to derive from renal cysts containing degraded blood. Lipids are also found in the urine of patients with primary abnormalities of lipid metabolism, such as Fabry's disease.

It is not currently known how lipid particles reach the final urine. It has been proposed that ultrafiltered lipids are reabsorbed by tubular cells but returned into the urine in the form of membrane-bounded lysosomal particles. Alternatively, tubular cells storing lipids may be sloughed off in the form of oval fat bodies [24]. The extent to which cholesterol within tubular cell is derived from reabsorbed ultrafiltered material or reflects, at least in part, local de novo synthesis of lipids [25] has not been clarified.

Fatty casts and *cholesterol crystals* are dealt with in pages 52 and 76.

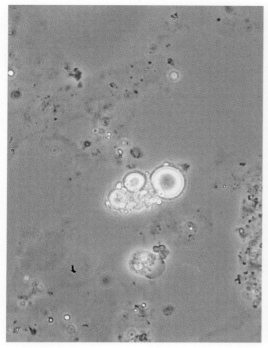

Fig. 2.51

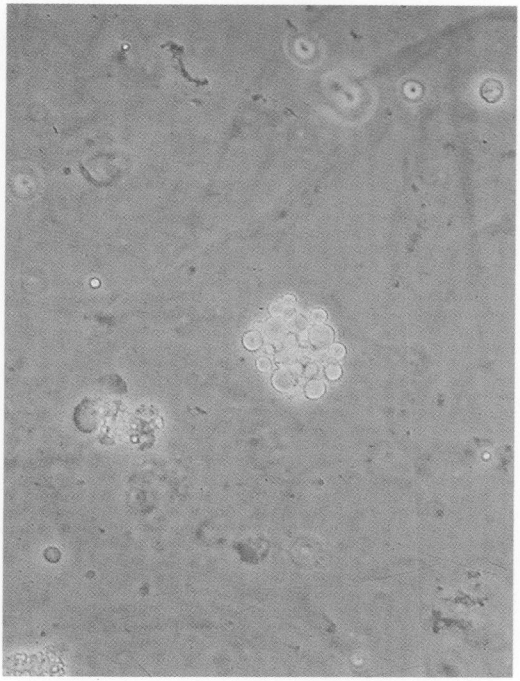

Fig. 2.52

Fig. 2.53

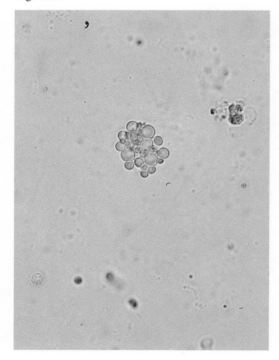

Fig. 2.51 *Free tiny lipid droplets and an oval fat body with lipid particles of variable size (phase contrast, X400).*

Fig. 2.52 *Oval fat body (phase contrast, X400).*

Fig. 2.53 *Oval fat body, the same as in figure 2.52, seen under the bright field microscope (X400).*

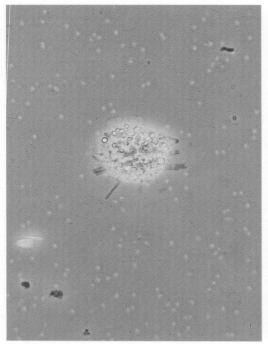

Fig. 2.54

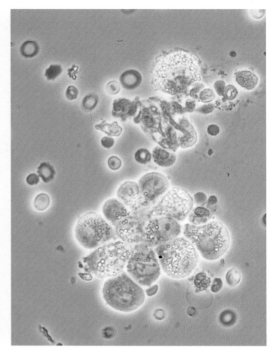

Fig. 2.55

Fig. 2.56

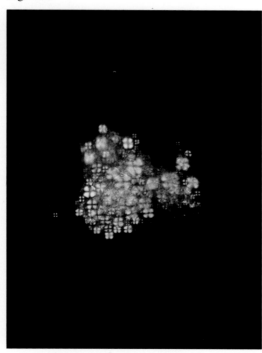

Fig. 2.54 *Oval fat body with protruding choles-terol plates (phase contrast, X400).*

Fig. 2.55 *Renal tubular cells partly laden with lipids (phase contrast, X400).*

Fig. 2.56 *Oval fat body under polarized light showing the typical "Maltese crosses" (X400).*

Casts

Cast are cylindrical in shape. They have rounded ends and are variable in diameter and length. The cylinders are replicas of the terminal part of the nephron. Their shapes and widths correspond to those of distal tubules and collecting ducts. Cylinder formation in the branching collecting duct is convincingly illustrated by the occasional finding of branched casts (figure 2.57). Studies using immunofluorescence have documented that the matrix of casts is composed of Tamm Horsfall protein [26] (figure 2.57) a glycoprotein synthesized by and secreted from the cells of the thick ascending limb of Henle's loop and the early distal convoluted tubule [27, 28]. Studies by electronmicroscopy have shown that Tamm Horsfall protein has a fibrillar structure. The fibrils are unbranched, of variable length and 9-15 nm in diameter. Under several physiological and pathological conditions, fibrils of Tamm Horsfall protein tend to aggregate and to interweave within the tubular lumen forming a gel. Sol-to-gel transformation is favored by low pH, high osmolality or high sodium concentration or by the interaction with substances such as myoglobin, hemoglobin etc. (figure 2.58). At first the gel is anchored to the tubular cells by fine fibrils, but subsequently it is washed out by tubular flow and is washed into the bladder in the form of a cast [29].

In bright field or phase contrast microscopy, casts are *simple* (i.e., hyaline casts) if they consist of Tamm Horsfall protein only or *complex* and of protean morphology, if they contain also granules, cells or other particles (figure 2.58). In fact, whatever elements are present in the tubular lumen during transition from the sol-to-gel phase will be trapped in the cast, e.g., filtered serum proteins, erythrocytes, leucocytes or epithelial cells. The final morphology of the casts also depends on the diameter of tubules in which the cast was formed. When the tubules are dilated, as in tubular atrophy or obstruction, large casts are seen in the urine. These casts are therefore indicative of renal failure ("renal failure casts"). Several types of casts can be found which differ in morphology, composition and diagnostic significance (table 2.2).

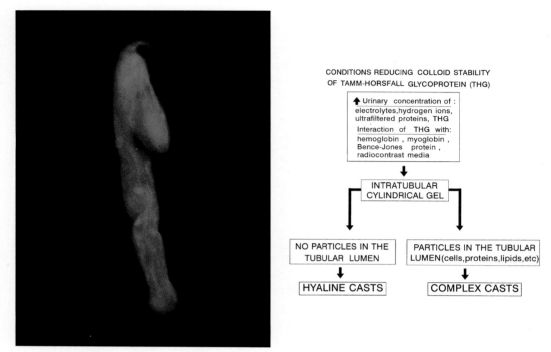

Fig. 2.57 *Branched cast stained with Tamm-Hors-fall antiserum (immunofluorescence microscopy, X250).*

Fig. 2.58 *Sequence of events leading to cast formation.*

CONDITIONS REDUCING COLLOID STABILITY
OF TAMM-HORSFALL GLYCOPROTEIN (THG)

⬆ Urinary concentration of :
electrolytes, hydrogen ions,
ultrafiltered proteins, THG
Interaction of THG with:
hemoglobin , myoglobin ,
Bence-Jones protein ,
radiocontrast media

INTRATUBULAR
CYLINDRICAL GEL

NO PARTICLES IN THE
TUBULAR LUMEN

PARTICLES IN THE TUBULAR
LUMEN (cells, proteins, lipids, etc)

HYALINE CASTS

COMPLEX CASTS

Table 2.2 Categories of casts

Type	Subtype
Hyaline	Compact
	Fibrillar
	Convoluted
Granular	Coarsely granular
	Finely granular
Waxy	
Cellular	Erythrocyte casts
	Leucocyte casts
	Tubular cell casts
Fatty	Lipid droplets
	Oval fat bodies
	Cholesterol crystals
With crystals	Calcium oxalate
	Amorphous urates or phosphates, etc
With microorganisms	Bacteria
	Fungi
Pigmented	Hemoglobin
	Myoglobin
	Bilirubin
Mixed	

Hyaline casts

Hyaline casts have a low refractive index and may be overlooked in bright field microscopy if they are not carefully looked for. They may display different shapes: compact, fibrillar, convoluted or wrinkled (figures 2.59-2.63). Scanning electronmicroscopic studies have shown that these different types simply reflect different degrees of interweaving of fibrils [30] (figure 2.64). In fibrillar casts the interweaving is loose, while in the compact casts it is tight. Wrinkling, instead, seems to be caused by dehydration and contraction of the fibrils or by degenerative processes. When hyaline casts are particularly wrinkled and the fibrils are loose it may be difficult to differentiate them from large mucus threads.

Hyaline casts can be seen in most renal diseases, alone or in combination with other types of casts. However, they are seen even in subjects without renal disease, particularly after physical exercise, during episodes of fever or dehydration or in patients with congestive heart failure. Imhof et al. [31] found transient abundant hyaline cylinders after single oral doses of furosemide (80-160 mg) or ethacrynic acid (50-100 mg).

Granular casts

Granular casts can easily be identified by bright field or phase contrast microscopy. They contain granules with variable number and shape, i.e., coarse or fine, dark or clear. Finely granular casts (figures 2.65-2.69) are common, while coarsely granular casts (figures 2.70 and 2.71) are more rare.

Coarse granules are thought to derive from degenerated cells, e.g., leucocytes [29]. The nature of fine granules seems to be different. In fact, immunofluorescence studies on urine of patients with proteinuria have shown that the fine granules contain several types of serum proteins [32, 33] and electron microscopy has demonstrated that granules resemble the cytoplasmic lysosomes of the tubular cells [34]. The fine granules may, therefore, be derived from ultrafiltered serum proteins which, after reabsorption by the proximal tubular cells are taken up by lysosomes and returned into the tubular lumen, where they are trapped in the matrix of forming casts. Finely granular casts can be observed, however, even in patients without proteinuria. It has been suggested that in these cases the granules result from cellular degeneration (figure 2.68).

Granular casts are usually not seen in the urines of subjects without renal disease. The finding of granular casts strongly indicates the presence of renal disease. Broad darkly granular casts are frequent in patients with renal failure.

Waxy casts

Waxy casts are easily recognizable by both bright field and phase contrast microscopy. These casts have a high refractive index, dark color and broad diameter. Their edges are hard, and are frequently, but not invariably, indented (figures 2.72-2.75). In electronmicroscopy, waxy casts also have a fibrillar core, as do other casts. However, their surface is modified by the appearance of "plates" of unknown composition [29] (figure 2.76). Waxy casts may be derived from cellular casts [35] or from hyaline casts that have been altered by urine products [29]. Waxy casts are typical of patients with renal failure and are frequent in glomerular diseases associated with rapid deterioration of the renal function.

Cellular casts

Casts may contain erythrocytes, leucocytes or tubular cells.

1) *Erythrocyte casts*: the erythrocytes within the casts usually appear as round cells without hemoglobin, but with regular and intact cytoplasmic membranes. Occasionally we have observed minor irregularities of the cell membrane, but never clearcut dysmorphic erythrocytes. The erythrocytes may be so tightly packed that the matrix can hardly be seen (figures 2.77 and 2.78). Alternatively, less erythrocytes are trapped and in these cases the casts can be correctly defined as erythrocyte-containing casts (figure 2.79). There are also transitions between erythrocyte casts and hemoglobin casts. Figures 2.80 and 2.81 illustrate transitions from intact to dissolving erythrocytes contained in casts within the tubular lumen. Erythrocyte and hemoglobin casts have the same clinical significance. Even the presence of a single erythrocyte or hemoglobin cast is a marker of glomerular bleeding. Therefore, they must be carefully looked for in the work-up of patients with hematuria. The diagnostic importance of these casts is considerable. They may be found even in patients with isolated hematuria and may then confirm the renal origin of hematuria.

Hemoglobin casts have a typical granular appearance, brownish color and hard and finely irregular edges (figures 2.82 and 2.83). They consist of either degenerated erythrocytes or entrapped ultrafiltered free hemoglobin (which occurs in patients with intravascular hemolysis).

Myoglobin casts are seen in the urines of patients with rhabdomyolysis. Their morphology is indistinguishable from that of hemoglobin casts (figure 2.84).

2) *Leucocyte casts*: these casts contain variable amounts of leucocytes. In most instances they are difficult to distinguish from tubular cells because the cells have degenerated. The smaller size of leucocytes, their finely granular appearance and their bright yellow color in phase contrast microscopy help to identify these elements (figures 2.85-2.87).

Leucocyte casts were once considered pathognomonic of acute upper urinary tract infection. They are also found, however, in patients with non-bacterial inflammation of the kidneys, e.g., in proliferative glomerulonephritis or acute interstitial nephritis.

3) *Tubular cell casts:* the tubular cells which are trapped in casts are usually round, larger than leucocytes and have large central or peripheral nuclei (figures 2.88-2.90). Conventionally these cells are called proximal tubular epithelial cells. It is impossible, however, to correctly identify cells originating from other tubular segments (see page 36).

Tubular cell casts can be found in the nephrotic syndrome, the nephritic syndrome and acute tubular necrosis.

Often it is not possible to differentiate between leucocytes and tubular cells and the casts are then simply called "cellular casts".

Fatty casts

When lipids are entrapped in the casts they may appear as droplets, as oval fat bodies or as cholesterol crystals. Their morphology and behaviour under polarized light do not differ from those of the same elements free in the urine (see page 46). The droplets may be rare, small and scattered, but even then they can be distinguished from the surrounding matrix since they are translucent (figure 2.91). In other instances, however, droplets may be so abundant that the matrix is completely masked (figures 2.92-2.95). Oval fat bodies are easy to identify within casts (figure 2.96) Cholesterol-containing casts are rare (figure 2.97).

Fatty casts are always associated with free lipids and are a typical marker of a heavy proteinuria.

Casts containing crystals and amorphous salts.

Crystals and amorphous salts strongly differ from cast matrix. Crystals and salts appear in clumps and identification is not difficult. Casts may contain any type of crystals and amorphous salts, but in our experience, calcium-oxalate containing casts have been the most frequent (figure 2.98).

The presence of these casts indicates that precipitation of crystals or salts has occurred in the tubules.

Casts containing microorganisms

Both bacteria and fungi have been observed in casts. According to Lindner et al. [36], *bacterial casts* have a granular or a mixed (granular and cellular) appearance. They have been observed only in patients with acute upper urinary tract infections. They are overlooked in bright field microscopy, but can be detected by phase contrast microscopy, light microscopy of stained sediments or electronmicroscopy. Although reported in the literature, they have not been identified in our laboratory.

Fungal casts have been found in the urines of patients with visceral candidiasis [37]. Their presence in immunocompromised patients strongly suggests renal parenchymal involvement.

Pigmented casts

Other pigments besides *hemoglobin* and *myoglobin* can cross the glomerular filter and stain casts or other elements of the urinary sediment.

Bilirubin casts. Casts of any type, i.e. hyaline, granular or cellular casts, may be stained by the typical yellow color of bilirubin (figure 2.99). Bilirubin casts may be observed when the concentration of direct, i.e., conjugated, bilirubin is increased.

Mixed casts

Different components may be present simultaneously in the same tubule, giving rise to mixed casts, e.g., hyaline-granular casts, granular-waxy casts, granular-cellular casts etc. (figures 2.100-2.103). Their origins are quite obvious and little is gained from more detailed classification.

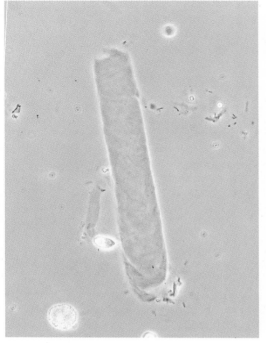

Fig. 2.59

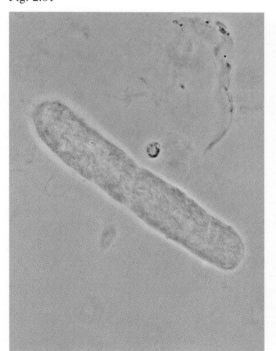

Fig. 2.61

Fig. 2.60

Fig. 2.62

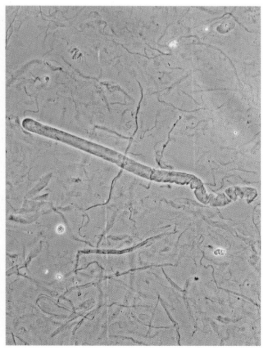

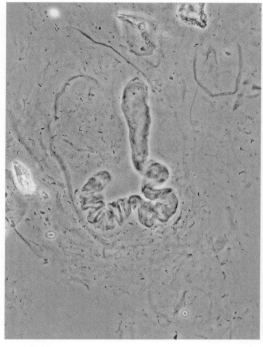

Fig. 2.63

Fig. 2.64

Fig. 2.65

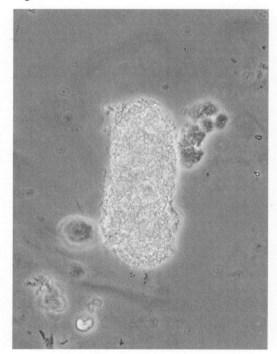

Fig. 2.59 *Compact hyaline cast (phase contrast, X400).*

Fig. 2.60 *Hyaline cast clearly showing the cylindrical shape which is the replica of the tubular lumen (phase contrast, X200).*

Fig. 2.61 *Fibrillar hyaline cast (phase contrast, X400).*

Fig. 2.62 *Compact hyaline cast with a convoluted extremity (phase contrast, X160).*

Fig. 2.63 *A markedly convoluted hyaline cast (phase contrast, X160).*

Fig. 2.64 *Scanning electronmicroscopy of a compact and a fibrillar hyaline cast (X1,500) (from Haber M.H.: The urinary sediment: a textbook atlas. Chicago: Am. Soc. Clin. Pathol., 1981. Used with permission).*

Fig. 2.65 *Finely granular cast (phase contrast, X400).*

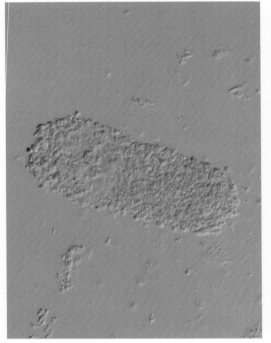

Fig. 2.66

Fig. 2.67

Fig. 2.68

Fig. 2.69

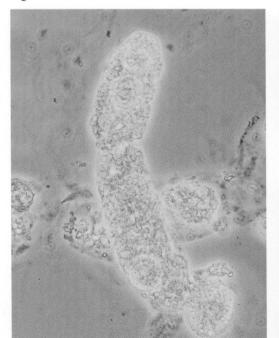

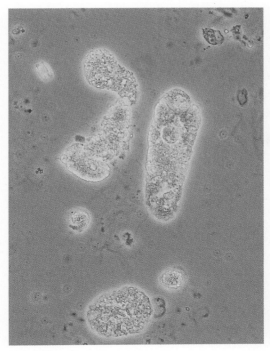

Fig. 2.70

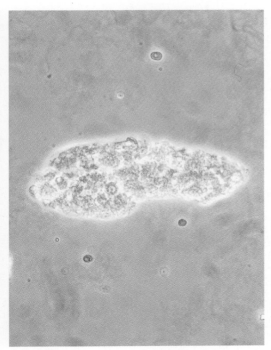

Fig. 2.71

Fig. 2.72

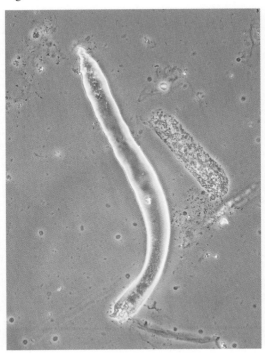

Fig. 2.66 *Finely granular cast under the interference contrast microscope (X256).*

Fig. 2.67 *Finely granular cast in which the hyaline matrix is still evident (phase contrast, X400).*

Fig. 2.68 *Granular cast which also contains degenerated granular cells. It is possible that the free granules of the cast were released during degeneration of the cells (phase contrast, X640).*

Fig. 2.69 *Scanning electronmicroscopy of a finely granular cast (X6,500) (from Haber M.H.: The urinary sediment: a textbook atlas. Chicago:Am. Soc. Clin. Pathol , 1981. Used with permission).*

Fig. 2.70 *Cast with fine and coarse granules (phase contrast, X400).*

Fig. 2.71 *Coarsely granular cast, clearly showing the cellular origin of the granules (phase contrast, X400).*

Fig. 2.72 *Large waxy cast compared with a finely granular cast (phase contrast, X160).*

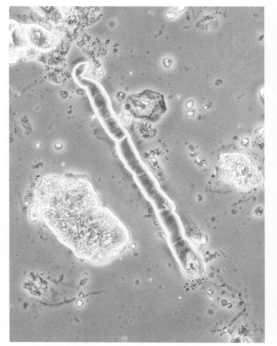

Fig. 2.73

Fig. 2.75

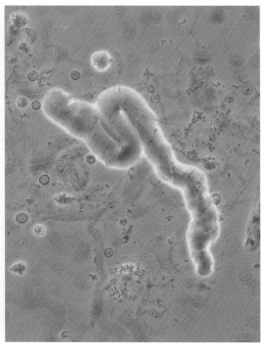

Fig. 2.74

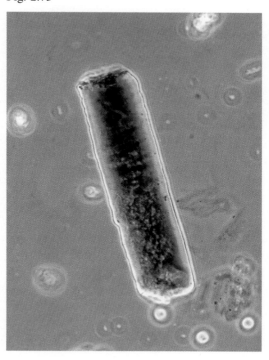

Fig. 2.73 *Waxy cast with indented edges (phase contrast, X200).*

Fig. 2.74 *Convoluted waxy cast (phase contrast, X256).*

Fig. 2.75 *Large and dark waxy cast with hard edges (phase contrast, X400)*

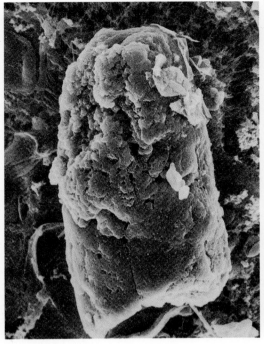

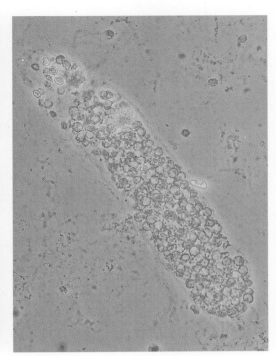

Fig. 2.76

Fig. 2.77

Fig. 2.78

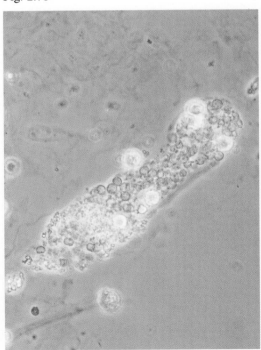

Fig. 2.76 *Scanning electronmicroscopy of a waxy cast, the surface of which also shows granules and amorphous material (X1,000) (from Haber M.H.: The urinary sediment: a textbook atlas. Chicago: Am. Soc. Clin. Pathol., 1981. Used with permission).*

Fig. 2.77 *Erythrocyte cast (phase contrast, X500).*

Fig. 2.78 *Erythrocyte cast also containing polymorphonuclear leucocytes, from a patient with acute postinfectious exudative glomerulonephritis (phase contrast, X400).*

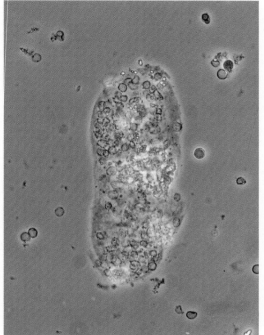

Fig. 2.79

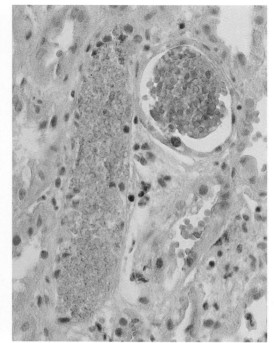

Fig. 2.80

Fig. 2.81

Fig. 2.82

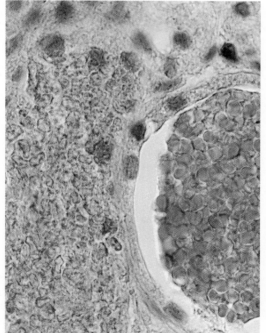

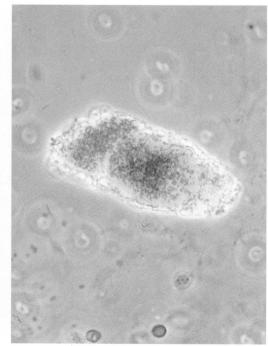

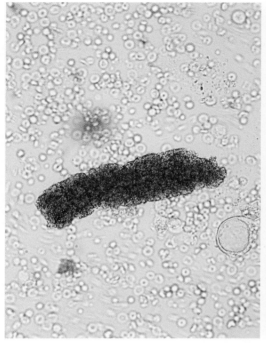

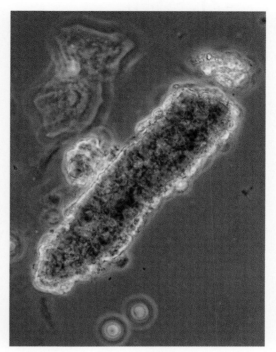

Fig. 2.83

Fig. 2.84

Fig. 2.85

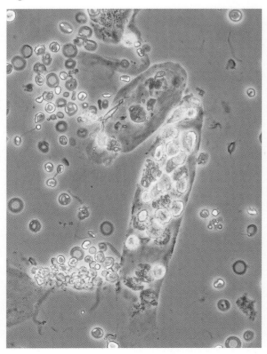

Fig. 2.79 *Cast containing erythrocytes, some granules and a few polymorphonuclear cells (phase contrast, X400).*

Fig. 2.80 *Intratubular erythrocyte (right) and hemoglobin (left) casts, observed in the renal biopsy of a patient with IgA nephropathy (AFOG stain, X400).*

Fig. 2.81 *The same picture as 2.80 at a higher magnification (X1,000) clearly shows the granular appearance of the hemoglobin cast.*

Fig. 2.82 *Hemoglobin cast, with the typical brownish color and granular appearance (phase contrast, X400).*

Fig. 2.83 *Hemoglobin cast as seen under the bright field microscope (X160).*

Fig. 2.84 *Myoglobin cast observed in the urine of a patient suffering from rhabdomyolisis due to heroin abuse (phase contrast, X400).*

Fig. 2.85 *Leucocyte-containing cast (phase contrast, X400).*

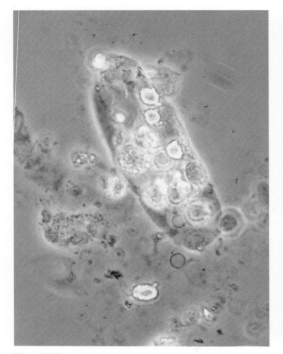

Fig. 2.86

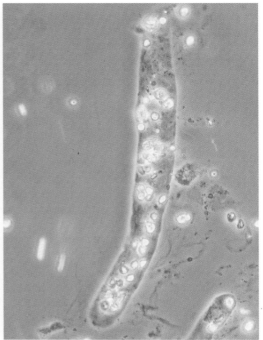

Fig. 2.87

Fig. 2.88

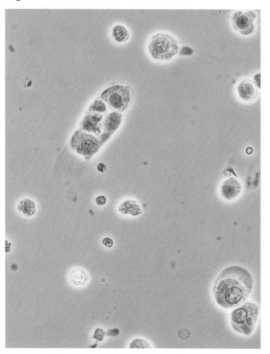

Fig. 2.86 *Leucocyte-containing cast (phase contrast, X400).*

Fig. 2.87 *Leucocyte-containing cast (phase contrast, X256).*

Fig. 2.88 *Cast containing several tubular cells. Other similar cells are free in the sediment (phase contrast, X400).*

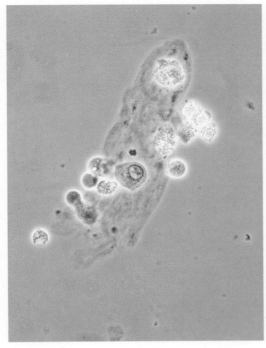

Fig. 2.89

Fig. 2.91

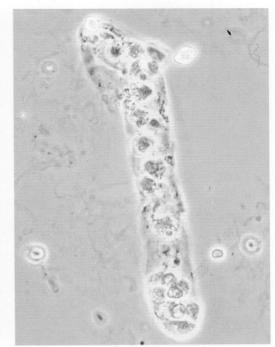

Fig. 2.90

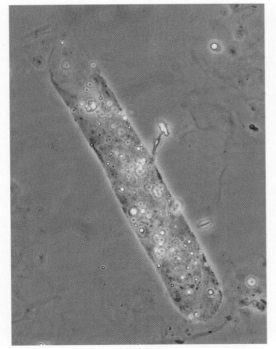

Fig. 2.89 *One ovoid tubular cell within the hyaline matrix of a cast (phase contrast, X400).*

Fig. 2.90 *Tubular cell-containing cast (phase contrast, X400).*

Fig. 2.91 *Hyaline cast containing several lipid droplets (phase contrast, X400).*

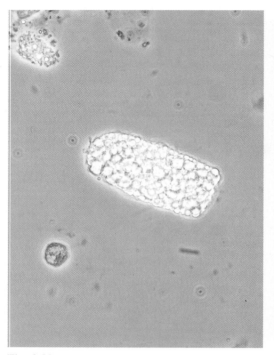

Fig. 2.92

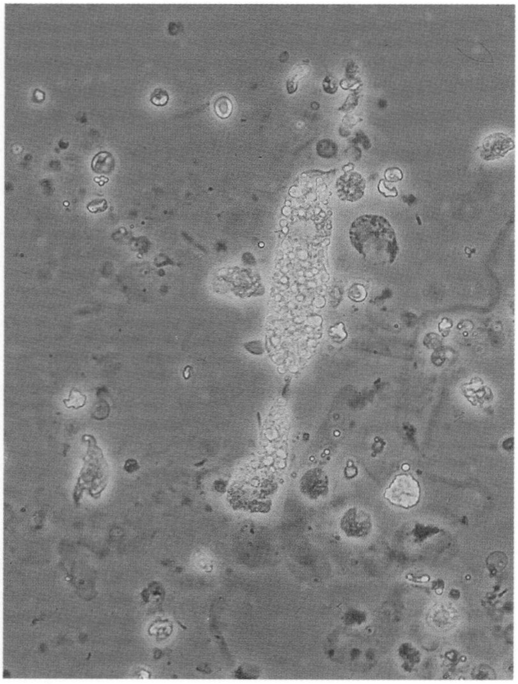

Fig. 2.94

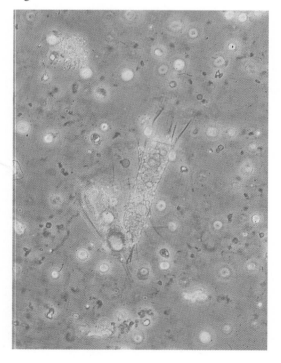

Fig. 2.93

Fig. 2.92 *Fatty cast (phase contrast, X400).*

Fig. 2.93 *Fatty cast (phase contrast, X400).*

Fig. 2.94 *Fatty cast with elongated spicules (cholesterol?) protruding from the edges (phase contrast, X200).*

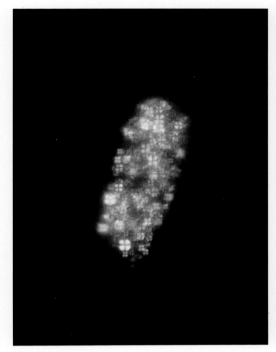

Fig. 2.95

Fig. 2.97

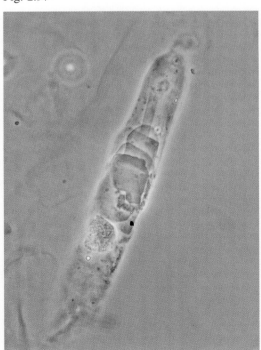

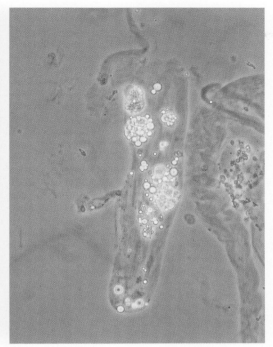

Fig. 2.96

Fig. 2.95 *Fatty cast as seen with polarized light (X640).*

Fig. 2.96 *Cast containing both lipid droplets and oval fat bodies (phase contrast, X400).*

Fig. 2.97 *Cast containing cholesterol crystals (phase contrast, X400).*

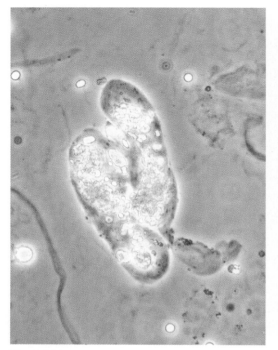

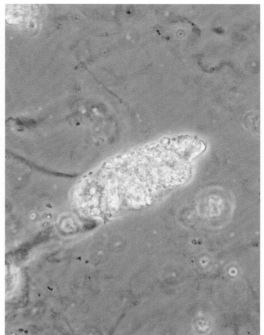

Fig. 2.98   Fig. 2.99

Fig. 2.100   Fig. 2.101

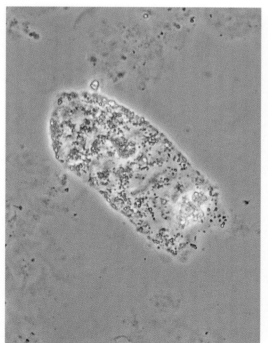

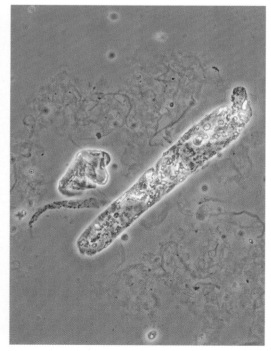

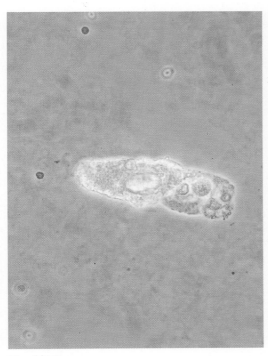

Fig. 2.98 *Two casts containing oval calcium oxalate crystals (phase contrast, X256).*

Fig. 2.99 *Cast with granules and cells stained by bilirubin (phase contrast, X500).*

Fig. 2.100 *Hyaline-granular cast (phase contrast, X400).*

Fig. 2.101 *Hyaline-granular-cellular cast (phase contrast, X256).*

Fig. 2.102 *Mixed cast containing both cells and pigmented granules (phase contrast, X256).*

Fig. 2.103 *Granular-waxy cast (phase contrast, X256).*

Fig. 2.102

Fig. 2.103

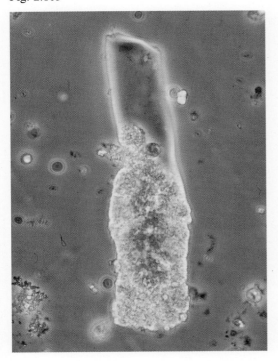

Cylindroids

There is no agreement about the definition and nature of cylindroids. According to Schreiner [38] and Graff [39], cylindroids are elongated elements with one rounded end, which resembles that of a cast, and another end which resembles a mucus thread. Adhering to this definition, in a prospective study of 600 sediments over a period of 4 months, we have found cylindroids in 90 samples from 79 patients. In almost all, i.e., 85 of 90 samples, cylindroids were associated with casts. Furthermore, we were able to observe hyaline, granular, cellular and lipid-containing cylindroids (figures 2.104-2.107). Furthermore, in cylindroids Tamm-Horsfall glycoprotein can be readily demonstrated by immunofluorescence. Consequently, we consider cylindroids to be one morphological variety of casts with the same diagnostic implications as casts.

Fig. 2.104 *Cylindroid (phase contrast, X160).*

Fig. 2.105 *Hyaline-granular cylindroid (phase contrast, X400).*

Fig. 2.106 *Cylindroid containing coarse granules, erythrocytes and other cells (phase contrast, X400).*

Fig. 2.107 *Cylindroid containing lipid droplets (phase contrast, X256).*

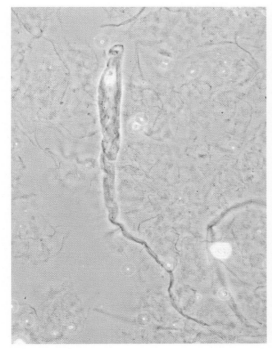

Fig. 2.104

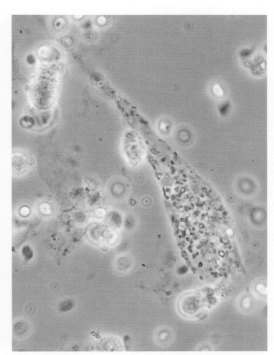

Fig. 2.105

Fig. 2.106

Fig. 2.107

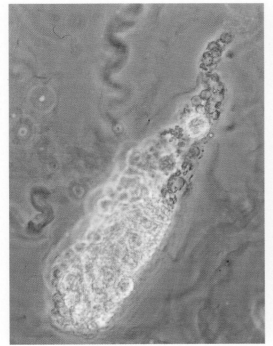

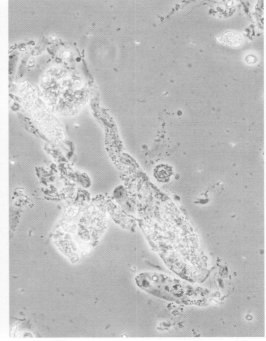

Pseudocasts

Many substances can clump and imitate the morphology of casts, for instance crystals, bacteria, cells, yeasts, mucus or contaminants (figures 2.108-2.110 and 2.124). Pseudocasts differ from casts for their edges, which are "harder" than those of the casts, and for their outline which may be irregular and not necessarily a replica of the tubular lumen. By immunofluorescence pseudocasts do not contain Tamm-Horsfall protein.

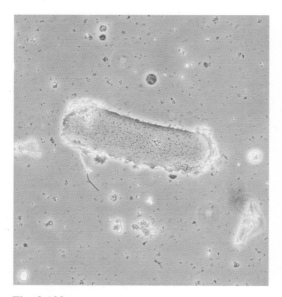

Fig. 2.108

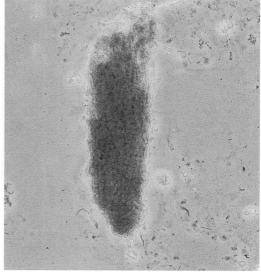

Fig. 2.109

Fig. 2.110

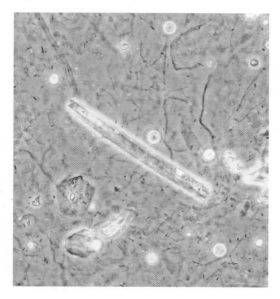

Fig. 2.108 *Pseudocast (resembling a hyaline cast) which is a calcium phosphate plate (phase contrast, X400).*

Fig. 2.109 *Pseudocast (resembling a hemoglobin cast) which is a cloth fiber (phase contrast, X256).*

Fig. 2.110 *Pseudocast (differing from a hyaline cast for the hard edges) due to a contaminant of undetermined origin (phase contrast, X200).*

Mucus

Mucus is frequently found in the urinary sediment. When studying 1,000 consecutive sediments, we found that mucus was absent from no more than 24% of the specimens, while some 38% contained mild to moderate amounts and the remaining 38% great quantities of mucus (table 2.3).

The extent to which mucus is derived from the secretion of accessory glands (Cowper's or Littré's glands in men; Skene's ducts in women) and to what extent it is derived from the glycocalyx of the transitional epithelial cell is unknown. It has been claimed that mucus is present more frequently in urines of women and that large amounts point to inflammation of the lower urinary tract or genital apparatus. In our series, mucus tended to be seen more frequently in men and large amounts of mucus were present in more than one third of the samples, despite no recognizable pathology. Moreover mucus is a frequent finding in the normal subject (see page 135).

Mucus has a low refractive index and is best seen by phase contrast microscopy. Usually it appears as ribbon-like threads with irregular contours and fibrillar structure (figure 2.111). The fibrils tend to be larger and more loosely textured than those seen in casts. Less frequently, mucus threads aggregate to form large masses (figure 2.112) or net works of fine fibrils. Occasionally threads of mucus resemble cylindroids.

Mucus has no diagnostic relevance *per se* but may affect evaluation of the urinary sediment. In fact, mucus threads may resemble cylindroids or hyaline casts. In such cases, one should look for indisputable casts, which solve the problem. Moreover, cells may be trapped in mucus (figure 2.113); this leads to grossly inhomogeneous distribution across the slide and may interfere with quantitation.

Table 2.3 Presence and amounts of mucus observed in 1,000 consecutive urinary sediments and its distribution in the two sexes

	Total	Women	Men
Number	1,000	550	450
	%	%	%
Absent	24	27	20
Modest	38	37.5	39
Marked	38	35.5	41

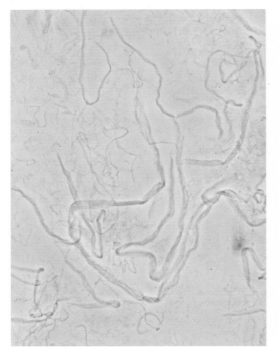

Fig. 2.111

Fig. 2.113

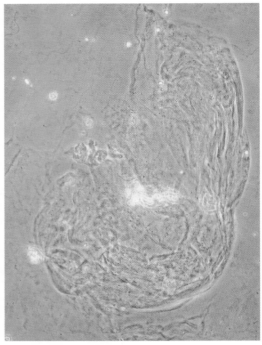

Fig. 2.112

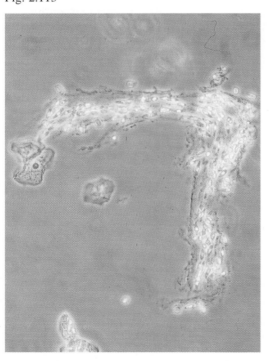

Fig. 2.111 *Ribbon-like mucus threads (phase contrast, X256).*

Fig. 2.112 *A large mass of mucus (phase contrast, X160).*

Fig. 2.113 *Mucus thread with entrapped cells (elongated polymorphonuclear leucocytes?) (phase contrast, X160).*

Crystals

Most crystals in the urine can be identified by their morphology, but this may be misleading since amorphous urates and phosphates are morphologically the same, hexagonal uric acid crystals may be similar to cystine crystals, bihydrated calcium oxalate crystals may be confused with triple phosphate. In these cases (i) knowledge of urinary pH (ii) birefringence under polarized light, and (iii) information about solubility may help to distinguish the different types of crystals (table 2.4).

Some crystals are seen only or predominantly in acid urine (e.g., urate) while others prevail in alkaline urine (e.g., phosphates). The presence of most types of urinary crystal is not pathological, while the presence of a few types is always indicative of a pathological condition, as shown in figure 2.114.

Table 2.4 Polarization and solubility properties of the urinary crystals

Crystals	Polarization	Solubility Yes	No
Acid urine			
Uric acid	Yes	Heat	Alcohol
Amorphous urates		Alkali	HCl, CH_3COOH
Calcium oxalate	*	HNO_3, NaOH HCl,	CH_3COOH
Hippuric acid	No	NaOH, hot H_2O Ether, alcohol	CH_3COOH
Cystine	Yes	HCl, NaOH NH_4OH	CH_3COOH Ether, alcohol Boiling H_2O
Tyrosine	No	NH_4OH, HCl NaOH, heat	Alcohol Ether CH_3COOH
Leucine	Yes	NaOH, Hot alcohol Hot CH_3COOH	Ether HCl Room temperature CH_3COOH
Cholesterol	Yes	$CHCl_3$ Ether Hot alcohol	Dilute acids Dilute alkalis Alcohol, H_2O
Alkaline urine			
Calcium phosphate	No	HCl, CH_3COOH	NaOH, heat
Triple phosphate	Yes		
Amorphous phosphate	No	HCl, CH_3COOH	NaOH, heat
Calcium carbonate	Yes	$HC+CO_2$ $CH_3COOH+CO_2$	NaOH, heat
Ammonium biurate	Yes	$NaOH+NH_3$, HCl CH_3COOH, heat	—

* = Bihydrated calcium oxalate crystals do not polarize in most instances. Occasionally they show a weak birefringence. Monohydrated calcium oxalate crystals, instead, are brightly birefringent.

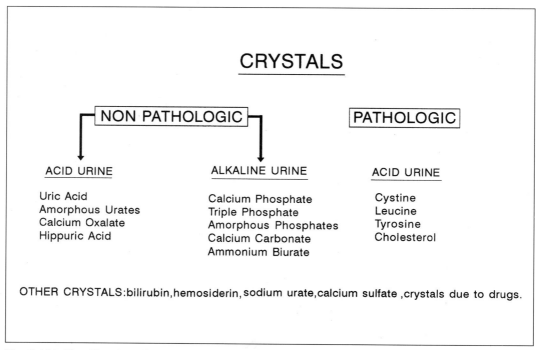

Fig. 2.114 *Classification of the crystals of the urinary sediment.*

Crystals found in acid urine

Uric acid crystals

Uric acid crystals are frequently observed. They are transparent and come in a wide variety of sizes and shapes (rhombs, barrels, rosettes, needles, six-sided plates, etc.). Their color is amber (figures 2.115-2.121). Under polarized light they are typically polychromatic (figures 2.122-2.124). When they are hexagonal, they resemble cystine crystals. Cystine crystals have irregular edges however, which is uncommon for uric acid crystals. Another possible misleading structure is glass slivers. These are colorless and are not birefringent. Uric acid crystals are dissolved by heating the sample or by adding alkali.

Unless freshly voided urine is examined, the presence of uric acid crystals has no clinical implications, since urates precipitate spontaneously when urine is left standing. However, when uric crystals are repeatedly found in freshly voided urine, are present in large quantities, or appear as large aggregates they may indicate primary or secondary hyperuricuria.

Amorphous urates

Amorphous urates are tiny colorless or dark granules which are present either singly or in clumps. They are morphologically indistinguishable from amorphous phosphates (figure 2.158). The latter, however, appear only in alkaline urine. Frequently very large amounts of amorphous urate mask all the other elements and after centrifugation a macroscopically pink to reddish sediment may be seen ("sedimentum lateritium"). Urates are birefringent under polarized light and disappear when the sample is heated or when alkali are added. They may be confused with cocci but cocci do not disappear after heating or after addition of alkali. The presence of amorphous urates is not pathological. They precipitate after voiding when urine has a low pH and is left standing at a low temperature.

Calcium oxalate crystals

These crystals are more frequent in acid urine, however they can be found at any pH. There are two types of calcium oxalate crystals, the bihydrated (Weddellite) and the monohydrated (Whewellite) variety. The former is colorless and bipyramidal in shape, of variable size. It may appear either singly or in aggregates (figures 2.125-2.127). Occasionally it can be confused with triple phosphate crystals, especially if the urine is alkaline, but their solubility properties are different (table 2.4). The monohydrated calcium oxalate crystals are colorless and have very different shapes (ovoids, biconcave disks, dumb-bell, etc.) (figures 2.128-2.132). When roundish, they can be confused with isomorphic erythrocytes, especially under the bright field microscope. Erythrocytes, however, are not refractile under polarized light and lyse when acetic acid is added.

The most frequent cause of calcium oxalate crystalluria is the ingestion of food with high oxalic acid content (tomatoes, spinach, oranges, asparagus, etc.) or large amounts of vitamin C. This type of crystalluria is typically transient and has no clinical significance. On the contrary, when the calcium oxalate crystals are persistently observed in freshly voided urine without relation to the ingestion of the before mentioned types of food, they may be indicative of oxaluria favoring the development of urolithiasis. In that case, quantitation of urinary excretion of oxalic acid is indicated (upper limit 40 mg/day). Rare causes of excessive oxaluria include intestinal disorders (enteric hyperoxaluria) and hereditary hyperoxaluria types I and type II, i.e., deficiency of the hepatic enzymes α-krtoglutarate: glyoxylate carboligase and D-glyceric dehydrogenase, respectively.

Hippuric acid crystals

These are uncommon. They have different shapes (rhombic plates, needles, prisms etc.) and may be colourless or yellow-brownish (figure 2.133). They are found after ingestion of fruits and vegetables containing great quantities of benzoic acid, but may also be observed in patients with liver disease or fever.

Cystine crystals

They are thin hexagonal colorless plates with irregular sides (figures 2.134-2.136). They can be either isolated, heaped upon one another, in clumps or in rosettes (figure 2.137). Under polarized light they are birefringent (figure 2.138). They are only seen in urine at pH 4. This pH is achieved by adding glacial acetic acid or by allowing refrigerated urine to stand overnight [40].

Cystine crystals may aggregate to form renal stones and are always indicative of hereditary disorders causing tubular wasting of cystine, particularly cystinuria.

Tyrosine and leucine crystals

The former appear as very thin needles, often aggregated in bundles or rosettes (see fig. 3.26 of ref. 39). They are found in patients with hepatic failure, e.g., acute hepatitis. Leucine crystals are oily-looking spheres with concentric striations (figures 2.139 and 2.140). Under polarized light they form pseudo-Maltese crosses. They are usually found in association with tyrosine and are seen in the same clinical conditions.

Cholesterol crystals

Cholesterol crystals appear as thin plates with well defined edges and corners. They are transparent and brownish. They may be either isolated or aggregates of variable sizes (figures 2.141-2.144). They are anistropic under polarized light and this feature is useful to differentiate them from talcum crystals. They are typical of the sediment in the nephrotic syndrome (see page 120), but they are found also in other conditions which are associated with lipiduria, e.g., chyluria due to the obstruction of the thoracic or abdominal lymphatic drainage.

Crystals found in alkaline urine

Phosphates

Phosphate crystals may be either calcium phosphates or triple phosphate.
Calcium phosphate crystals can also be observed in neutral or mildly acidic urine. They can be non-polarizing needles, pointed prisms or rosettes (figures 2.145-2.148) or thin large plates with granular surfaces (figures 2.149 and 2.150). They do not necessarily have pathological significance, but if excessive they may be indicative of stone formation.
Triple phosphate crystals, i.e., magnesium-ammonium-phosphate, are transparent birefringent prisms. In most instances they have a coffin lid appearance (figures 2.151-2.155), while in other cases they are trapezoidal (figures 2.156 and 2.157). Most frequently they precipitate when the urine pH is rendered alkaline by urea-splitting bacteria. This may happen either in infected freshly voided urine or in urine with bacterial overgrowth after prolonged standing.

Amorphous phosphates

Amorphous phosphates are microscopically identical to amorphous urates (figure 2.158). These latter, however, are birefringent under polarized light, while phosphates are not. Also amorphous phospathes can be very abundant and mask all other elements of the sediment. They may be mistaken for cocci and precipitate spontaneously at low temperatures. Unlike urates, phosphates yield a white macroscopically visible sediment on the bottom of the tube after centrifugation. They have no pathologic significance and are frequently found in healthy individuals during the so-called "alkaline tide", i.e., excretion of alkaline urine following ingestion of food.

Calcium carbonate crystals

They are pleomorphic, being spheres, dumb-bells or coarse granules, which appear often in aggregates (figure 2.159). Calcium carbonate crystals are birefringent under polarized light. They are found after ingestion of large amounts of vegetables and have no clinical implications.

Ammonium biurate crystals

These crystals are rare. They have a yellow to brownish color and have a spherical shape, with or without spicules (figures 2.160-2.162). In most instances they do not have clinical implications. However, since their precipitation is favored by splitting of urea, they may point to the presence of urinary tract infection.

Other rare crystals

Bilirubin: yellowish-brown granules, needles or plates. They may be seen in the urine of patients with jaundice.

Hemosiderin: reddish brown granules very similar to amorphous urates or phosphates. They may be found in the urine of patients with intravascular hemolysis.

Sodium urate: these crystals precipitate in acid urine as needles, prisms or amorphous material and do not have clinical implications.

Calcium sulfate: these crystals, which are clinically unrelevant, are morphologically identical to calcium phosphate crystals. Unlikely these however, calcium sulfate precipitates in acid urine.

Crystals due to drugs: see page 135.

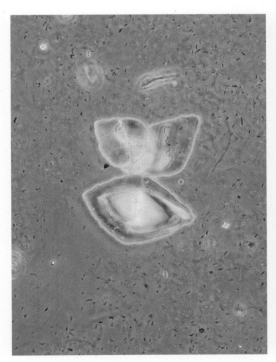 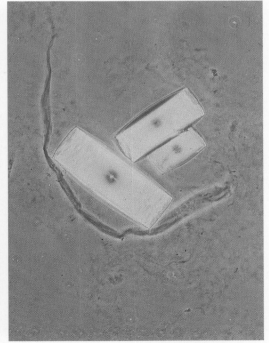

Fig. 2.115 *Rhomboid uric acid crystals. Note the amber color (phase contrast, X400).*

Fig. 2.116 *Biconvex uric acid crystals (phase contrast, X400).*

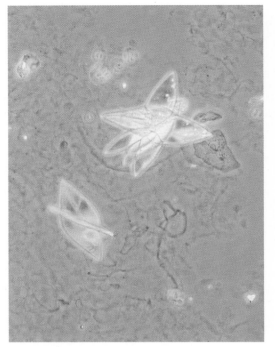

Fig. 2.117

Fig. 2.119

Fig. 2.120

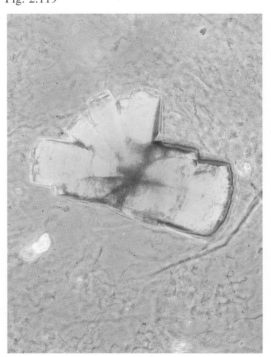

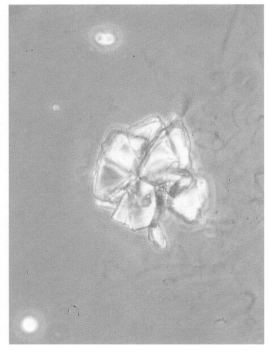

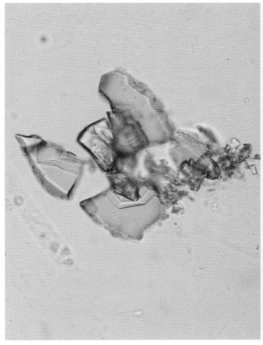

Fig. 2.121

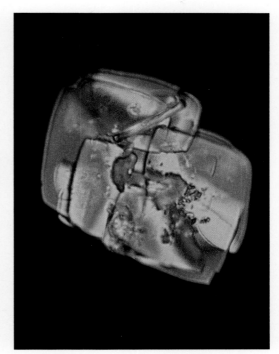

Fig. 2.122

Fig. 2.123

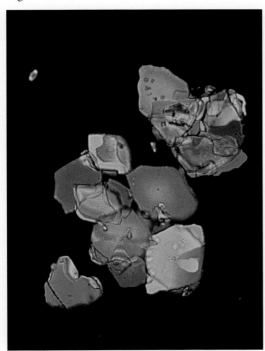

Fig. 2.117 *Uric acid crystals forming a rosette (phase contrast, X160).*

Fig. 2.118 *Barrel-shaped uric acid crystal (bright field, X400).*

Fig. 2.119 *Large uric acid crystal (phase contrast, X160).*

Fig. 2.120 *Cluster of uric acid crystals (phase contrast, X256).*

Fig. 2.121 *Irregular uric acid crystals resembling glass slivers (bright field, X250).*

Fig. 2.122 *Rhomboid uric acid crystals as seen under polarized light (X400).*

Fig. 2.123 *Rhomboid and hexagonal uric acid crystals under polarized light (X250).*

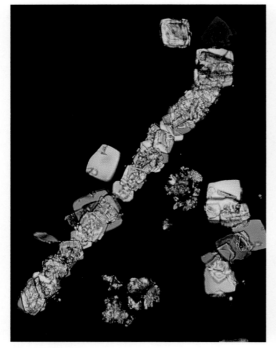

Fig. 2.124

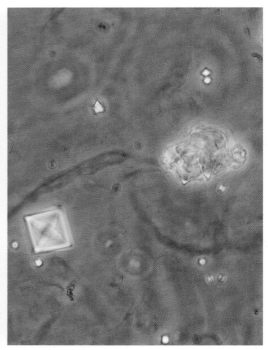

Fig. 2.125

Fig. 2.126

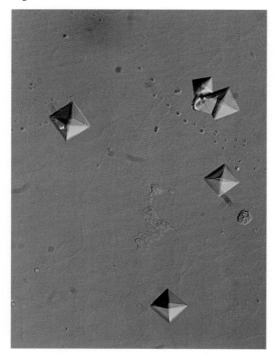

Fig. 2.124 *Uric acid crystals clustered to form a pseudocast (polarized light, X250).*

Fig. 2.125 *Bihydrated calcium oxalate crystals: isolated (left) and in a small cluster (right) (phase contrast, X640).*

Fig. 2.126 *Typical bipyramidal calcium oxalate crystals (interference contrast, X640).*

Fig. 2.127

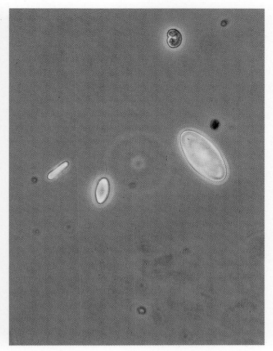

Fig. 2.128

Fig. 2.129

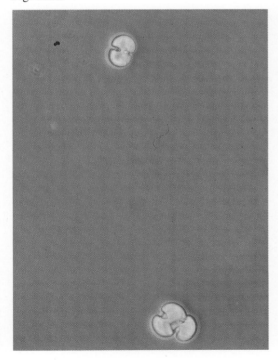

Fig. 2.127 *Bipyramidal and ovoid calcium oxalate crystals (interference contrast, X256).*

Fig. 2.128 *Ovoid monohydrated calcium oxalate crystals (phase contrast, X640).*

Fig. 2.129 *Biconcave crystals of monohydrated calcium oxalate (phase contrast, X400).*

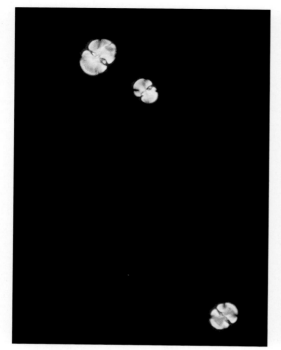

Fig. 2.130

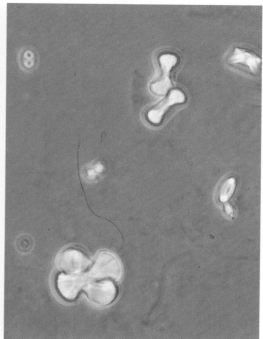

Fig. 2.131

Fig. 2.132

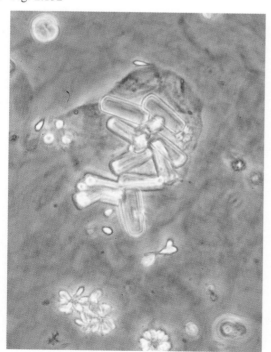

Fig. 2.133

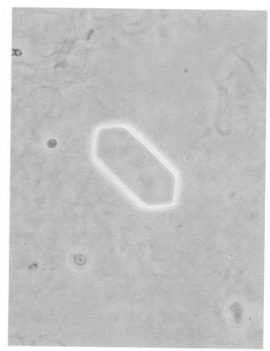

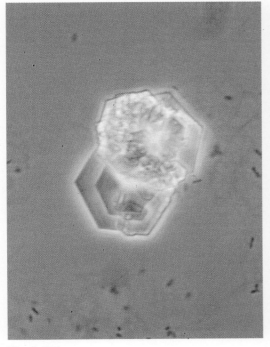

Fig. 2.134

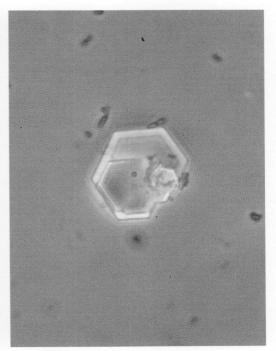

Fig. 2.135

Fig. 2.136

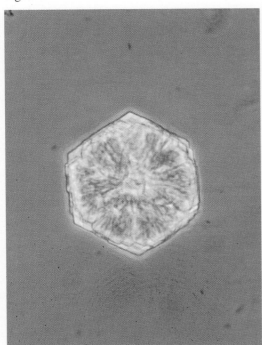

Fig. 2.130 *Birefringent biconcave crystals of monohydrated calcium oxalate under polarized light (X400).*

Fig. 2.131 *Dumb-bell-shaped calcium oxalate crystals (phase contrast, X400).*

Fig. 2.132 *Rod-shaped monohydrated calcium oxalate crystals (phase contrast, X500).*

Fig. 2.133 *Hexagonal plate of hippuric acid (phase contrast, X400).*

Fig. 2.134 *Cystine crystals (phase contrast, X500).*

Fig. 2.135 *Birefringent hexagonal crystals of cystine (phase contrast, X400).*

Fig. 2.136 *A cystine crystal displaying a rosette-like appearance inside a hexagon (phase contrast, X640).*

84

G.B. Fogazzi, P. Passerini, C. Ponticelli, E. Ritz

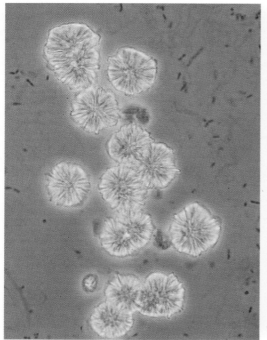

Fig. 2.137

Fig. 2.138

Fig. 2.139

Fig. 2.140

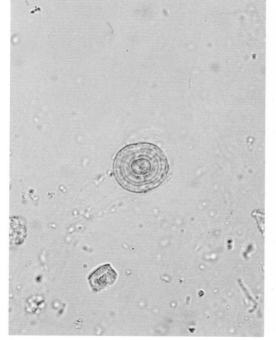

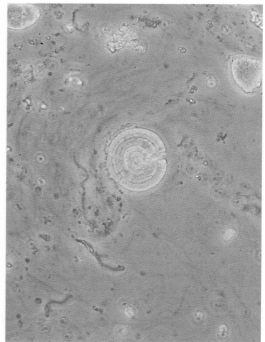

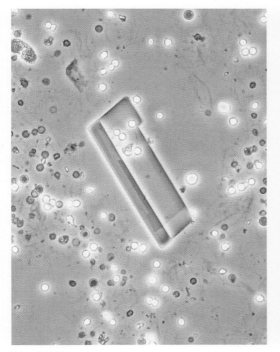

Fig. 2.141

Fig. 2.143

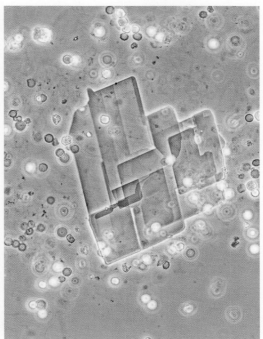

Fig. 2.142

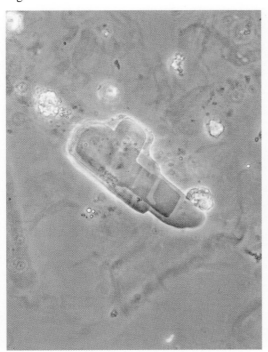

Fig. 2.137 *Cystine crystals in rosettes (phase contrast, X256).*

Fig. 2.138 *Cystine crystals in rosettes under the polarized light (X500).*

Fig. 2.139 *Leucine crystal (bright field, X400).*

Fig. 2.140 *Leucine crystal (phase contrast, X400).*

Fig. 2.141 *Cholesterol crystal (phase contrast, X200).*

Fig. 2.142 *Large cluster of cholesterol crystals (phase contrast, X400).*

Fig. 2.143 *Cholesterol crystal with rounded edges (phase contrast, X400).*

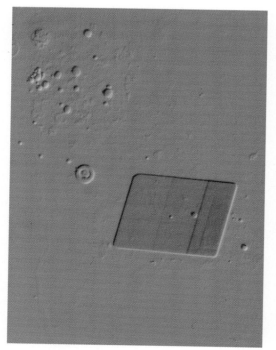

Fig. 2.144

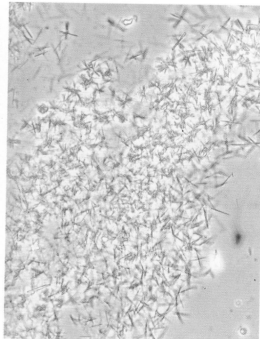

Fig. 2.145

Fig. 2.146

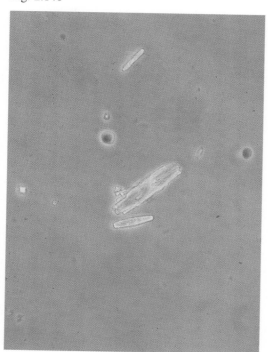

Fig. 2.144 *A cholesterol crystal under the interference contrast microscope. Note also a dysmorphic erythrocyte and lipid droplets (X800).*

Fig. 2.145 *Large clump of calcium phosphate needles (phase contrast, X256).*

Fig. 2.146 *Calcium phosphate prisms (phase contrast, X400).*

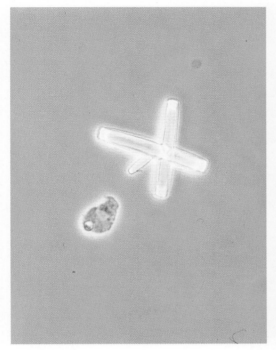

Fig. 2.147

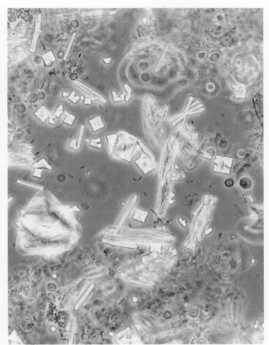

Fig. 2.148

Fig. 2.149

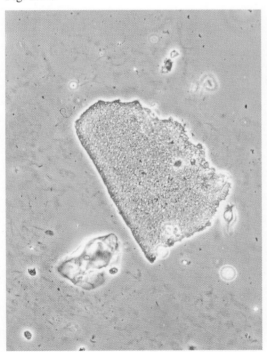

Fig. 2.147 *Calcium phosphate prisms forming a rosette (phase contrast, X400).*

Fig. 2.148 *Calcium phosphate pointed prisms (isolated and in clumps) mixed with bipyramidal calcium oxalate crystals (phase contrast, X400).*

Fig. 2.149 *Calcium phosphate plate (phase contrast, X400).*

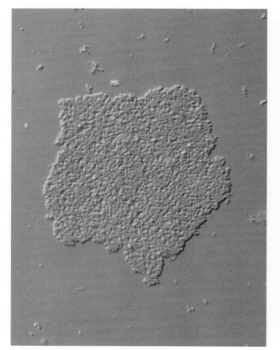

Fig. 2.150

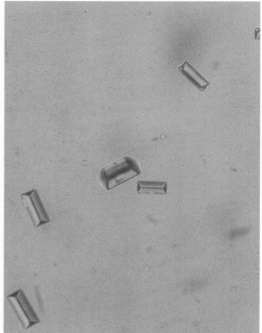

Fig. 2.151

Fig. 2.152

Fig. 2.153

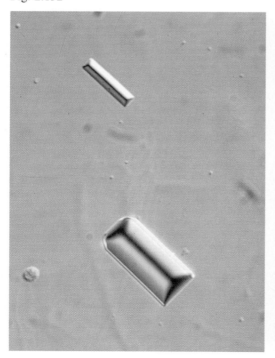

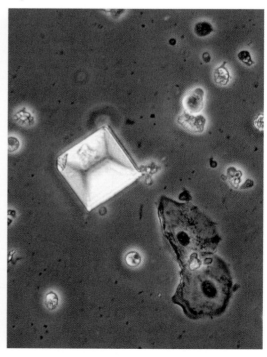

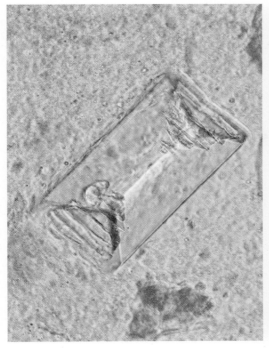

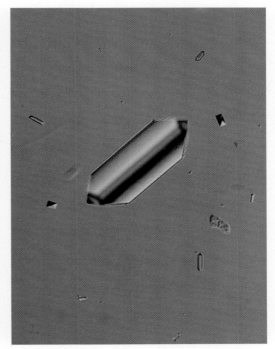

Fig. 2.154

Fig. 2.155

Fig. 2.156

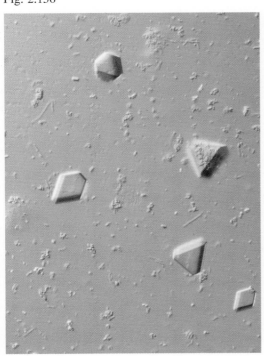

Fig. 2.150 *The granular appearance of the calcium phosphate plates is clearly seen by the interference contrast microscope (X500).*

Fig. 2.151 *Triple phosphate crystals with the typical appearance of coffin lids (bright field, X400).*

Fig. 2.152 *Triple phosphate crystals (interference contrast, X400).*

Fig. 2.153 *Square-shaped triple phosphate crystal (phase contrast, X256).*

Fig. 2.154 *Large triple phosphate crystal (bright field, X640).*

Fig. 2.155 *Triple phosphate crystal with pointed extremities (interference contrast, X400).*

Fig. 2.156 *Trapezoidal triple phosphate crystals (interference contrast, X400).*

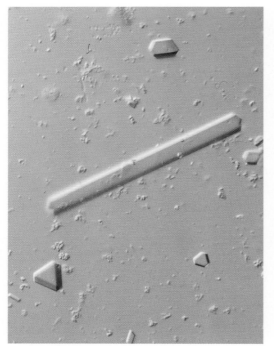

Fig. 2.157

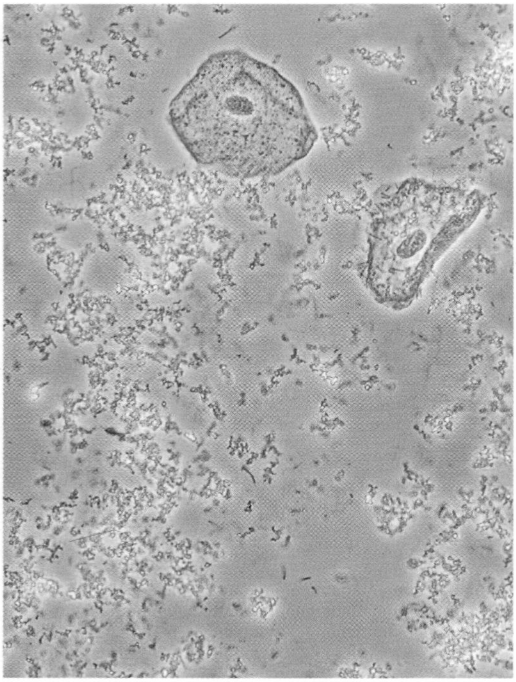

Fig. 2.158

Fig. 2.159

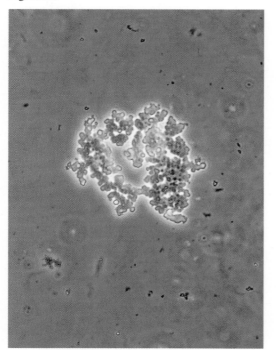

Fig. 2.157 *Trapezoidal and rod-like crystals of triple phosphate (interference contrast, X400).*

Fig. 2.158 *Amorphous phosphates. Only the urinary pH and polarization properties differentiates amorphous phosphates from amorphous urates (phase contrast, X400).*

Fig. 2.159 *Calcium carbonate crystals (phase contrast, X400).*

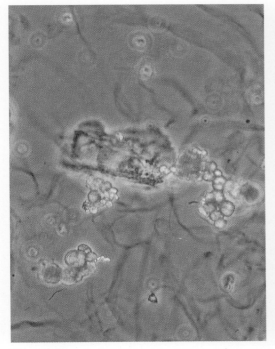

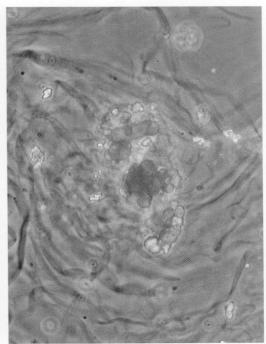

Fig. 2.160

Fig. 2.161

Fig. 2.162

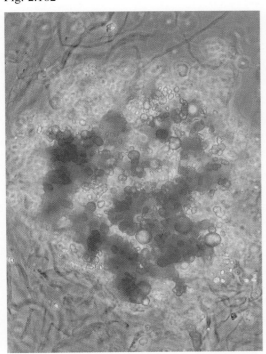

Fig. 2.160 *Spherical ammonium biurate crystals in clumps (phase contrast, X400).*

Fig. 2.161 *Ammonium biurate crystals (phase contrast, X400).*

Fig. 2.162 *Ammonium biurate crystals (phase contrast, X640).*

Organisms

Several organisms can be identified in urinary sediments (table 2.5).

Table 2.5 Microorganisms found in the urinary sediment

Bacteria	Rods and cocci
Yeasts	Candida
Protozoa	Trichomonas vaginalis
Parasites	Schistosoma haematobium
	Enterobius vermicularis

Bacteria

Bacteria are not present in uninfected urine, but urinary sediments, if not properly handled, may acquire abundant bacteria when the urine is collected, handled or analyzed under non-sterile conditions. If there is a major delay between micturition and examination, bacterial growth may occur. Urinary infection must be suspected if bacteria can clearly be identified in non-contaminated freshly voided urine, particularly if numerous leucocytes are also present (figure 2.163). Contamination is more likely if many squamous cells are present.

In phase contrast microscopy, bacteria appear as dark grey or black particles. *Rods* may be isolated, in pairs or in long chains (figure 2.164) and the same is true for *cocci* (figure 2.165). Rods and cocci are easy to distinguish, but sometimes cocci are difficult to distinguish from amorphous crystals. Brownian movement of cocci may be useful for this differentiation. Bacteria may adhere to epithelial cells (figure 2.48). Adhesion of bacteria to cells, i.e., colonisation, is thought to be an important step in ascending urinary tract infection. Bacteria, when abundant, may clump into masses of variable size (figure 2.166).

In acute upper urinary tract infections with parenchymal involvement ("acute pyelonephritis"), bacterial casts and casts containing a mixture of cells and bacteria have been described by others, but we have been unable to observe them (see page 53).

Yeasts

Yeasts are unicellular organisms which reproduce by budding and separation of daughter cells. *Candida* are the most frequent yeasts found in the urine. There are more than 80 candida species but only a few of them are pathogenic for humans. Of these, *candida albicans* is the most commonly found.

Genital candidiasis is the most frequent cause of candida in the urine. This reflects contamination of the urine. Candida, however, can also grow in the urinary tract, mostly in patients with diabetes mellitus, structural abnormalities of the urinary tract, indwelling catheters, prolonged antibiotic treatment or immunosuppression. Under these conditions, candida in urine may either be asymptomatic or invasive. Invasive candida infection may cause urethritis or lower and upper urinary tract infection. Occasionally fungus balls form, i.e. macroscopically visible mycelia.

There is no agreement concerning the best method of urine collection to evaluate candiduria. Midstream specimens seem to be more reliable than random urine specimens. According to Dreetz and Fetchik [41] catheterization or, preferably, suprapubic puncture are advisable to verify the presence of candida in the urine. One unresolved problem is distinguishing between invasive urinary tract infections and colonization. It has been claimed that the presence of pseudomycelia, i.e., chains of elongated unseparated yeasts in specimens obtained by catheterization or bladder puncture is indicative of urinary tract infection, but this view is not universally accepted. The presence of pyuria may help to make the distinction, but several cases of definite infection have been observed without pyuria. Investigation for antibody coated yeasts has been proposed to distinguish between lower and upper urinary tract infection, but this test is unreliable. The presence of candidal casts is a useful sign pointing to renal infection [37]. These casts are observed in preparations stained by Papanicolaou's method, but cannot be detected in wet preparations under the bright field microscope. It is possible that fungus casts may be identified under the phase contrast microscope, but we did not have the opportunity to observe them.

Candida appear as refractile pale-green cells with smooth and well defined walls. The size and shape of the cells, i.e. elongated, ovoid or spherical (figures 2.167 and 2.168) is characteristic of the particular candida species. The cells of candida albicans are ovoid, while those of candida kruzei are elongated, but differentiation of candida species exclusively on the basis of microscopy is unreliable. Round yeast cells resemble erythrocytes, but candida cells are more refractile and often nucleated. After urine has been left standing, abundant pseudomycelia are often observed (figure 2.169). Rarely yeasts may be seen in clumps (figure 2.170).

Trichomonas vaginalis

Trichomonas vaginalis is a protozoon which is found in the genital and urinary tracts of both sexes. It is the most frequent cause of vaginitis in women and of urethritis in men. Trichomonas vaginalis in the urine indicate contamination by genital secretions. In the typical case of trichomonas vaginitis, such genital secretions will also contain leucocytes, bacteria and/or candida albicans. Trichomonas vaginalis is oval or round, is of variable size but mostly barely larger than a leucocyte and has an oval indistinct nucleus and four flagella. One additional flagellum, bent backward, is linked to the body by an undulating membrane (figures 2.171 and 2.172). When alive, trichomonas vaginalis can be readily identified by the motility of the flagella and the rapid and irregular movements of the body. Dead trichomonas vaginalis are difficult to distinguish from leucocytes.

Schistosoma haematobium

Infection with schistosoma haematobium (or urinary Bilharziosis) is endemic in the Middle East, particularly in the Nile valley, the Arabian peninsula and West Africa, but it is also observed in East and South Africa.

The infection is transmitted to humans by certain fresh-water snails which, after infection by miracidia, deliver large numbers of cercariae. These penetrate into the human body through the skin. They transform into mature adult parasites in the portal system and reach the venous plexus around the lower end of the ureters and the urinary bladder. Here adult parasites mate and produce eggs which pass from the venules of the vesical plexus into the bladder wall and the lower end of the ureters. The eggs stimulate the formation of vesical and ureteral granulomata, which cause mucosal hyperemia, ulcers, polypoid vegetations and give rise to hematuria, proteinuria, obstructive uropathy, urinary tract infection or urolithiasis.

Although serological procedures have become available, the diagnosis of schistosoma haematobium infection still heavily relies on observation of the eggs in the urine. Urinary microscopy is important not only for diagnosis, but counting of eggs in the urinary sediment yields an estimate of the severity of the infection. Hematuria and proteinuria are also related to the severity of infection [42]. The eggs of schistosoma haematobium can be better visualized and counted after urine is filtered through paper or Nucleopore filters. Unstained or stained preparations can then be examined [43]. Since excretion of the eggs is maximal around midday, collection of urine at midday is recommended. Mature eggs of schistosoma haematobium measure about 140×50 µm and are spindle shaped with a rounded anterior and a conical posterior end tapering into a delicate terminal spine (figure 2.173).

Because of immigration and tourism, cases of schistosoma haematobium infection can be seen outside the endemic areas.

Enterobius (oxyuris) vermicularis

The pinworm Enterobius vermicularis is a parasite mostly of children, causing a generally benign infection which is seen throughout the world. The parasite inhabits the cecum and the colon in which it lives adhering to the intestinal mucosa. When gravid, the females detach from the intestinal mucosa and migrate towards the rectum. Once they reach the anus they crawl onto the perianal and perineal skin, where they deposit the eggs and die. The diagnosis is made by placing scotch tape over the perianal and perineal skin and watching for pinworms and their ova to attach. In the female, pinworms can reach the vagina and internal genitalia. It has been proposed that pinworms covered by enteric bacteria migrate through the urethra into the bladder. This may explain the high prevalence of urinary tract infection in girls infected with enterobius vermicularis [44].

Occasionally enterobius vermicularis are found in the urine either as contaminants, from the anus, genitalia or urethra or as parasites of the bladder. Ova measure about 25×50 µm, have one flat side while the other is rounded, and have a double-layered wall (figure 2.174).

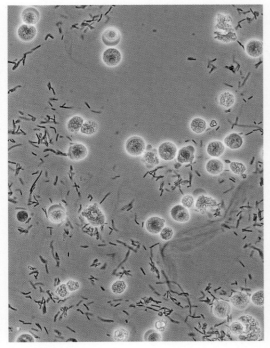

Fig. 2.163

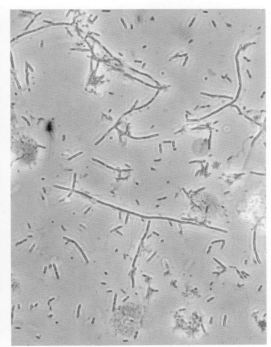

Fig. 2.164

Fig. 2.165

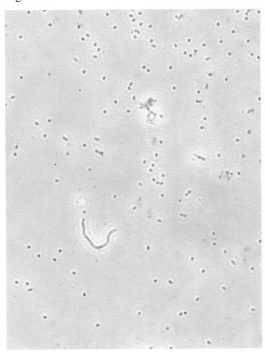

Fig. 2.163 *Rods mixed with polymorphonuclear leucocytes (phase contrast, X400).*

Fig. 2.164 *Long chains of rods intermingled with isolated cocci (phase contrast, X640).*

Fig. 2.165 *Cocci isolated, in pairs and in chains (phase contrast, X640).*

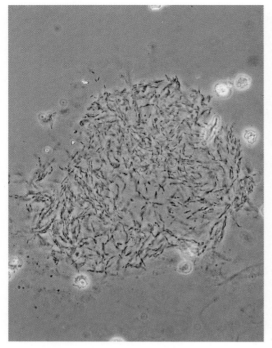

Fig. 2.166

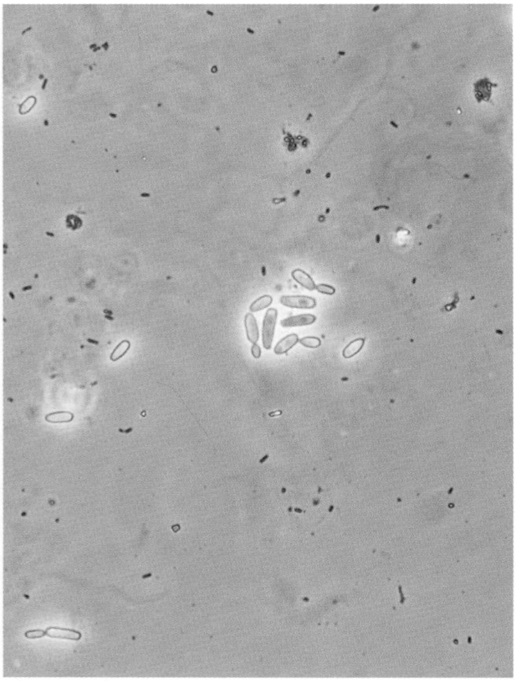

Fig. 2.167

Fig. 2.168

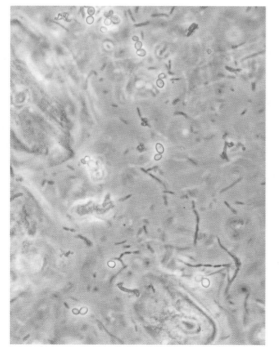

Fig. 2.166 *Large mass of cocci (phase contrast, X400).*

Fig. 2.167 *Elongated candidae with buds (phase contrast, X640).*

Fig. 2.168 *Ovoid candidae with buds (phase contrast, X640).*

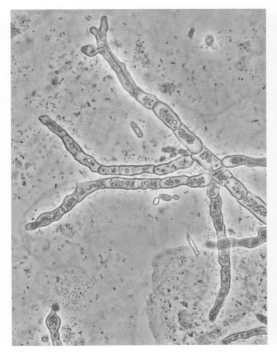

Fig. 2.169

Fig. 2.171

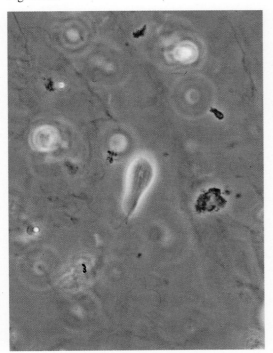

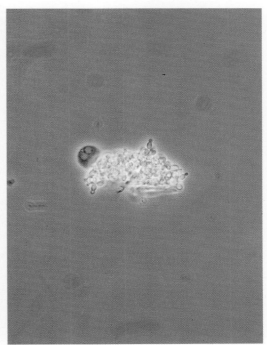

Fig. 2.170

Fig. 2.169 *Pseudomycelia (phase contrast, X640).*

Fig. 2.170 *Candidae in a clump (phase contrast, X256).*

Fig. 2.171 *Pear-shaped trichomonas vaginalis (phase contrast, X400).*

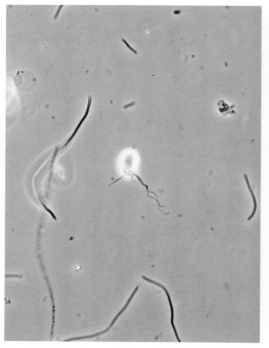

Fig. 2.172

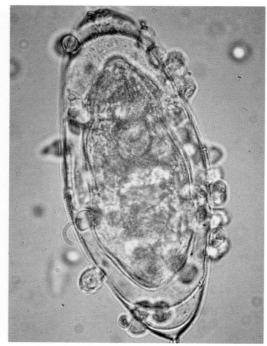

Fig. 2.173

Fig. 2.174

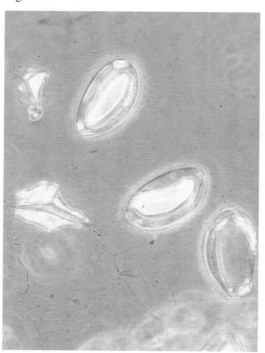

Fig. 2.172 *Dead trichomonas vaginalis with evident flagella (phase contrast, X400).*

Fig. 2.173 *Egg of schistosoma haematobium (courtesy of Professor Ivo Decarneri, Pavia) (bright field, X400).*

Fig. 2.174 *Eggs of enterobius vermicularis (courtesy of Doctor Laura Bossi, Milano) (phase contrast, X400).*

Contaminants

The term "contaminant" applies to all elements which enter the urine once it has left the bladder. The possible contaminants are numerous and can come from the patient, the laboratory or the environment (table 2.6). The contaminants are not diagnostic *per se*, but must be correctly identified to avoid misinterpretation. Contamination should be avoided by proper urine collection and clean working conditions.

Table 2.6 Principal sources of contamination of the urine

Patient	Contamination originating from Laboratory	Environment
Erythrocytes#	Starch	Pollen granules
Leucocytes#	Glass fragments	Plant cells
Squamous cells	Air bubbles	Fungal spores
Bacteria#		Fibers
Spermatozoa		
Trichomonas vaginalis		
Pubic hair		
Phthiriasis		
Feces		
Enterobius vermicularis		
Cloth fibers		
Talcum		
Oil		

Contaminants when deriving from urethra or genital secretions.

Contaminants originating from the patient

Most contaminants of the urinary sediment, e.g. *erythrocytes*, *leucocytes* and *squamous cells* are due to genital secretions. In women, erythrocytes can enter the urine during menstruation or periovulatory bleeding. Contamination by erythrocytes and leucocytes may also be the result of gynecological disorders. In men, contamination can result from urethritis or balanoposthitis. *Bacteria, yeasts* and *trichomonas vaginalis* may contaminate the urine of patients with genital infections, e.g., vaginitis. *Spermatozoa* may be present in the urine after intercourse, even in urines of women (figure 2.175). *Pubic hair* may also be found in the urine, but this should cause no diagnostic difficulty; we have even seen *phthiriasis* in urinary specimens. Contaminants may also originate from the gastrointestinal tract. A rare cause is the presence of fistulae between the intestine and the urinary tract, e.g., in Crohn's disease, in malignancy or after irradiation. *Feces* appear as particles of variable shape and size which may contain tissue strands, muscle and/or vegetable fibers (figure 2.176). The rare occurrence of *enterobius vermicularis* has been mentioned above (figure 2.174) (see page 94).
Other contaminants originating from the patient are *cloth fibers*. These can still exhibit the texture of the cloth and be colored. They are either flat or cylindrical (figures 2.177-2.179). In the latter case they may be confused with casts. The contours of the casts, however, are less hard and more regular. At high magnification, casts frequently show finely fibrillar structure which the fibers lack. *Talcum* powder, when applied to the genital area may find its way into the urine. Talcum particles are crystalline in structure. Their morphology varies from pin-like

particles to large multilayered irregular bodies (figure 2.180). Talcum crystals may occasionally resemble cholesterol crystals from which they can be differentiated because they are not transparent and not birefringent under polarized light. Talcum crystals may also resemble glass slivers. *Oil droplets* are round particles of variable diameter resembling lipid droplets (figure 2.181). Under polarized light, however, oil droplets do not show "Maltese crosses" as lipid particles do. Contaminating oil droplets are derived from lubricants used in urological maneuvers.

Contaminants originating in the laboratory

Starch is a frequent contaminant of the urinary sediment and comes from the dusting powder used for the gloves worn in the laboratory or for surgery. Starch particles are translucent, roundish to polygonal, with a nucleus-like center. They are colorless under the bright field microscope and bright yellow under the phase contrast microscope (figure 2.182). Under polarized light, starch granules resemble birefringent lipid droplets, from which they can be differentiated by their larger size and by the asymmetrical dark cross (figure 2.183). *Glass fragments* are another frequent contaminant. They are transparent particles of irregular shape with hard edges (figure 2.184). At times it may be difficult to differentiate glass from the irregular uric acid crystals. The amber color of the uric acid and the lack of birefringence of glass allow correct identification. Glass slivers are due to microfragments released from glass containers or coverslips. *Air bubbles* are an artefact rather than a contaminant. Very exceptionally, Co_2 may be formed in the urines of diabetic patients by gas-forming bacteria. Air bubbles have often, but not always, a round shape and dark double contours (figure 2.185). They result from air bubbles in the resuspended urine or from air trapped between the slide and the coverslip.

Contaminants originating in the environment

Several elements from environmental sources, especially from the air, may contaminate the urine while it is handled in the laboratory. Even though there is no way to completely avoid this type of contamination, it should be clear that the risk increases with time when urine is kept in containers without cover.

Pollen granules are occasionally found in urinary sediments. The morphology of pollens greatly varies according to their nature, as it is well shown in figures 2.186 and 2.187. *Plant cells* have distinct double-layered walls surrounding a large nucleus. *Fungal spores*, e.g., alternaria (figure 2.188), helminthosporium (figure 2.189), epicoccum (figure 2.190) and cladosporium (figure 2.191) can also contaminate the urine.

In a study of 1,600 urinary sediments conducted over one year period, we have found that fungal spores, especially alternaria, appear in the urine almost throughout the year, with a peak from June through October. The spores are usually present in soil and plants and reach the laboratory through the air. Table 2.7 shows the criteria to differentiate contaminants from other elements of the urinary sediment.

Table 2.7 Characteristic features for differentiating contaminants in the urine sediment

Trichomonas vaginalis	vs	Leucocytes	Flagella and motility
Cylindrical cloth fibers	vs	Casts	Hard edges
			Lack of finely fibrillar structure
Talcum powder	vs	Cholesterol	Lack of transparency
			Lack of birefringence
Oil droplets	vs	Lipids	Lack of birefringence
Starch	vs	Lipids	Asymmetrical cross under polarized light
Glass fragments	vs	Uric acid crystals	Colorless
			Lack of birefringence

Tables 2.8 and 2.9 show the meaning of some elements of the urinary sediment in relationship with some diseases of the kidney and with the site of the damage.

Table 2.8 Elements of the urinary sediment that are pathognomonic or suggestive for specific renal disease

Element	Disease
Eosinophils>5%	Acute interstitial nephritis
Lymphocytes	Acute cellular rejection of transplant
Dysmorphic erythrocytes	Glomerular bleeding#
Erythrocyte casts	Glomerular bleeding#
Hemoglobin casts	Glomerular bleeding or hemoglobinuria
Leucocyte casts	Renal parenchymal infection or inflammation
Cystine crystals	Cystinuria

Dysmorphic erythrocytes and erythrocyte casts are also found in interstitial nephritis. This seems to indicate that there are postglomerular sites of entry as well.

Table 2.9 Elements of the urinary sediment indicating the site of damage

Element	Location
Dysmorphic erythrocytes	Glomerulus (and tubule)
Tubular cells	Tubule
Casts	Tubule
Transitional cells	Urothelium

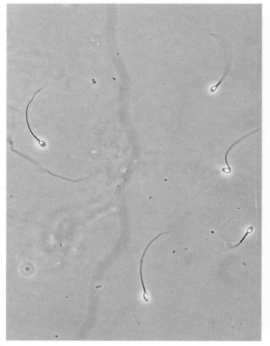

Fig. 2.175

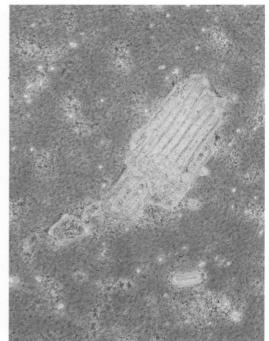

Fig. 2.176

Fig. 2.177

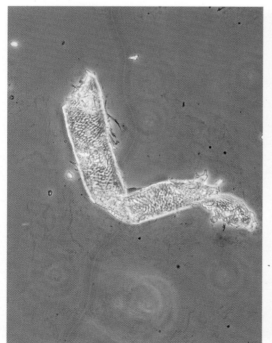

Fig. 2.178

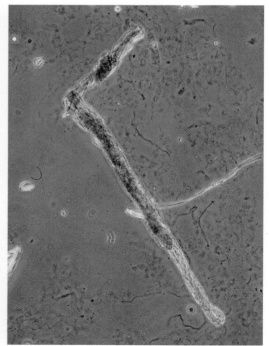

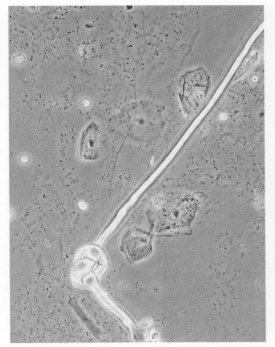

Fig. 2.179

Fig. 2.181

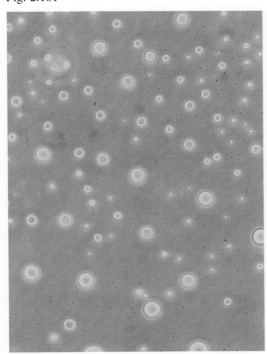

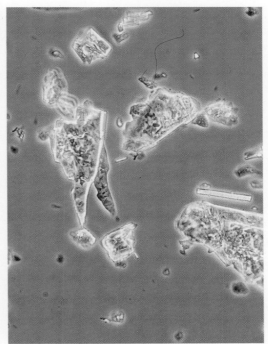

Fig. 2.180

Fig. 2.175 *Spermatozoa (phase contrast, X400).*

Fig. 2.176 *Muscle fibers due to fecal contamination of the urine (phase contrast, X160).*

Fig. 2.177 *Cloth fiber. The cloth texture is clearly visible (phase contrast, X160).*

Fig. 2.178 *Blue cloth fiber (phase contrast, X160).*

Fig. 2.179 *Knotted cloth fiber (phase contrast, X160).*

Fig. 2.180 *Talcum crystals (phase contrast, X400).*

Fig. 2.181 *Oil droplets (phase contrast, X160).*

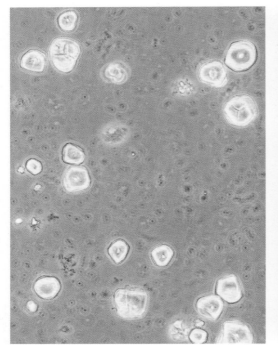

Fig. 2.182

Fig. 2.183*

Fig. 2.184

Fig. 2.185

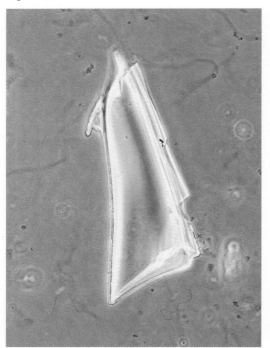

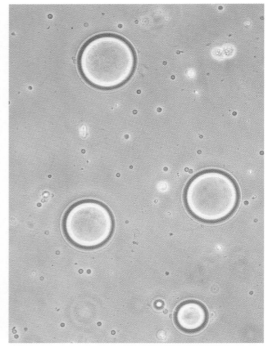

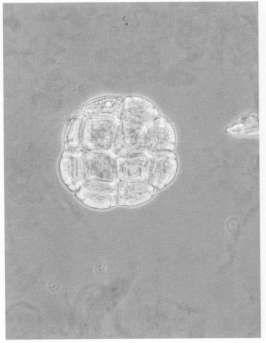

Fig. 2.186

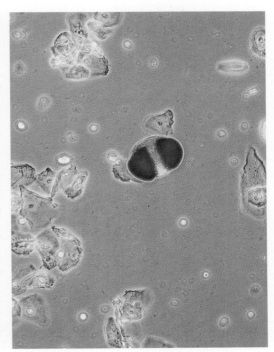

Fig. 2.187

Fig. 2.188

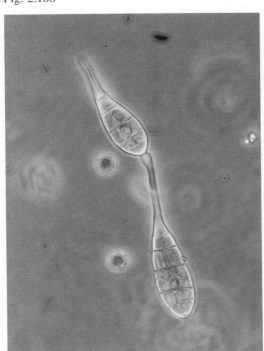

Fig. 2.182 *Starch crystals (phase contrast, X400).*

Fig. 2.183 *Polarized starch particles. Note the asymmetrical Maltese crosses (X250).*

Fig. 2.184 *Glass sliver (phase contrast, X400).*

Fig. 2.185 *Air bubbles (phase contrast, X400).*

Fig. 2.186 *Pollen (family Leguminosae) (phase contrast, X400).*

Fig. 2.187 *Pollen (family Pinaceae) (phase contrast, X160).*

Fig. 2.188 *Alternaria (phase contrast, X400).*

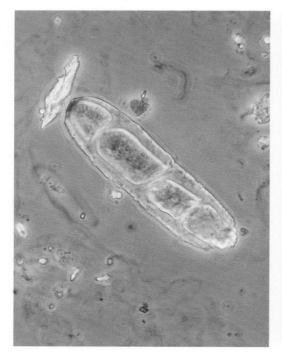

Fig. 2.189

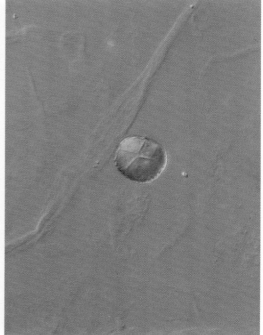

Fig. 2.190

Fig. 2.191

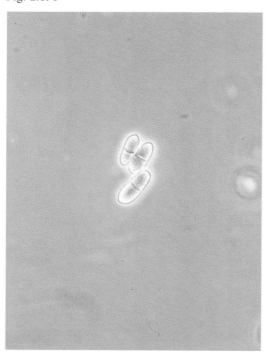

Fig. 2.189 *Helminthosporium (phase contrast, X400).*

Fig. 2.190 *Epicoccum (interference contrast, X500).*

Fig. 2.191 *Cladosporium. Note the similarity to elongated candidae (phase contrast, X400).*

References

[1] FAIRLEY K.F., BIRCH D.: *Hematuria: a simple method for identifying glomerular bleeding.* Kidney Int., 21: 105-8, 1982.

[2] FASSET R.G., HORGAN B.A., MATHEW T.H.: *Detection of glomerular bleeding by phase-contrast microscopy.* Lancet, i: 1432-4, 1982.

[3] RIZZONI G., BRAGGION F., ZACCHELLO G.: *Evaluation of glomerular and nonglomerular hematuria by phase-contrast microscope.* J. Pediatr., 370-4, 1983.

[4] DeE SANTO N., NUZZI F., CAPODICASA G., et al.: *Phase-contrast microscopy of the urine sediment for the diagnosis of glomerular and nonglomerular bleeding — data in children and adults with normal creatinine clearance.* Nephron, 45: 35-9, 1987.

[5] ROTH S., RENNER E., RATHERT P.: *Microscopic hematuria: advances in identification of glomerular dysmorphic erythrocytes.* J. Urol., 146: 680-4, 1991.

[6] VENKAT RAMAN G., PEAD L., MASKELL R.: *A blind controlled trial of phase-contrast microscopy by two observers for evaluating the source of haematuria.* Nephron, 44: 304-8, 1986.

[7] THIEL G., BIELMANN D., WEGMANN W., et al.: *Glomeruläre Erythrozyten im Urin: Erkennung und Bedeutung.* Schweiz med. Wochenschr., 116: 790-7, 1986.

[8] TOMITA M., KITAMOTO Y., NAKAYAMA M., et al.: *A new morphological classification of urinary erythrocytes for differential diagnosis of glomerular hematuria.* Clin. Nephrol., 37: 84-9, 1992.

[9] KÖHLER H., WANDEL E., BRUNCK B.: *Acantocyturia — A characteristic marker for glomerular bleeding.* Kidney Int., 40: 115-20, 1991.

[10] VAN ISEGHEM P., HAUGLUSTAINE D., BOLLENS W.: *Urinary erythrocyte morphology in acute glomerulonephritis.* Brit. Med. J., 287: 1183, 1983.

[11] FOGAZZI G.B., MORONI G.: *Ematuria glomerulare e non glomerulare.* G. Ital. Nefrol., 1: 45-9, 1984.

[12] SCHUETZ E., SCHAEFER R.M., HEIDBREDER E., et al.: *Effect of diuresis on urinary erythrocyte morphology in glomerulonephritis.* Klin. Wochenschr., 63: 575-7, 1985.

[13] SERRA A., TORGUET P., ROMERO R.R., et al.: *Normal urinary red blood cell morphology in segmental necrotizing glomerulonephritis.* Nephron, 59: 351-2, 1991.

[14] FOGAZZI G.B., BANFI G., PONTICELLI C.: *Acute tubular necrosis caused by gross hematuria in a patient with focal and segmental necrotizing glomerulonephritis.* Nephron, 61: 102-5, 1992.

[15] TRUNG L.J., HIROYOSHI W., HIROSHI M., et al.: *Mechanism of hematuria in glomerular disease.* Nephron, 35: 68-72, 1983.

[16] SCHRAMEK P., MORITSCH A., HASCHKOWITZ H., et al.: *In vitro generation of dysmorphic erythrocytes.* Kidney Int., 36: 72-7, 1989.

[17] CORWIN H.L., HABER M.H.: *The clinical significance of eosinophiluria.* Am. J. Clin. Pathol., 88: 520-2, 1987.

[18] WILSON D.M., SALAZER T.L., FARKOUH M.E.: *Eosinophiluria in atheroembolic renal disease.* Am. J.Med., 91: 186-9, 1991.

[19] KRISHNA G.G., FELLNER S.K.: *Lymphocyturia: an important diagnostic and prognostic mar er in renal allograft rejection.* Am. J. Nephrol., 2: 185-8, 1982.

[20] SANDOZ P.F., BIELMANN D., MIHATSCH M.J., et al.: *Value of urinary sediment in the diagn sis of interstitial rejection in renal transplants.* Transplantation, 41: 343-8, 1986.

[21] RIVAS MANGA M.F., CIFUENTES DELATTE L.: *Histiocitos en la orina.* Rev. Clin. Espan., 131: 293-8, 1973.

[22] BRADEN L., SANCHEZ P.G., FITZGIBBON J.P., et al.: *Urinary doubly refractile lipid bodies in nonglomerular renal diseases.* Am. J. Kidney Dis., 11: 332-7, 1988.

[23] DUNCAN K.A., CUPPAGE F.E., GRANTHAM J.J.: *Urinary lipid bodies in polycystic kidney disease.* Am. J. Kidney Dis., 5: 49-53, 1985.

[24] ZIMMER J.G., DEWEY R., WATERHOUSE C., et al.: *The origin and nature of anisotropic urinary lipids in the nephrotic syndrome.* Ann. Intern. Med., 54: 205-14, 1961.

[25] COMINGS D.E.: *Anisotropic lipids and urinary cholesterol excretion.* JAMA, 183: 126, 1963.

[26] McQUEEN E.G.: *Composition of urinary casts.* Lancet, 1: 397-8, 1966.

[27] HOYER J.R., SEILER M.W.: *Pathophysiology of Tamm-Horsfall protein.* Kidney Int., 16: 279-89, 1979.

[28] KUMAR S., MUCHMORE A.: *Tamm-Horsfall protein-uromodulin (1950-1990).* Kidney Int., 37: 1395-401, 1990.

[29] HABER M.H., LINDNER L.E.: *The surface ultrastructure of urinary casts.* Am. J. Clin. Pathol., 68: 547-52, 1977.

[30] LINDNER L.E., HABER M.H.: *Hyaline casts in the urine: mechanism of formation and morphologic transformations.* Am. J. Clin. Pathol., 80: 347-52, 1983.

[31] IMHOF P.R., HUSHAK J., SCHUMANN G., et al.: *Excretion of urinary casts after administration of diuretics.* Brit. Med. J., 2: 199-202, 1972.

[32] RUTECKI G.J., GOLDSMITH C., SCHREINER G.E.: *Characterization of proteins in urinary casts*. New Engl. J. Med., 284: 1049-52, 1971.

[33] ORITA Y., IMAI N., UEDA N., et al.: *Immunofluorescent studies of urinary casts*. Nephron, 19: 19-25, 1977.

[34] LINDNER L.E., VACCA D., HABER M.H.: *Identification and composition of types of granular urinary casts*. Am. J. Clin. Pathol., 80: 353-8, 1983.

[35] ADDIS T.: *Renal failure casts*. JAMA, 84: 1013, 1925.

[36] LINDNER L.E., JONES R.N., HABER M.H.: *A specific urinary cast in acute pyelonephritis*. Am. J. Clin. Pathol., 73: 809-11, 1980.

[37] GREGORY M.C., SCHUMANN G.B., SCHUMANN J.L., et al.: *The clinical significance of candidal casts*. Am. J. Kidney Dis., 4: 179-84, 1984.

[38] SCHREINER G.E.: *The identification and clinical significance of casts*. Arch. Intern. Med., 99: 356-69, 1957.

[39] GRAFF L.: *A handbook of routine urinalysis*. Philadelphia: Lippincot, 98, 1983.

[40] HALPERIN E.C., THEIR S.O.: *Cystinuria*. In: Coe F.L., Brenner B.M., Stein J.H. eds. *Nephrolithiasis*. New York: Churchill Livingstone, 208-30, 1980.

[41] DREETZ D.J., FETCHICK R.: *Fungal infections of the kidney and urinary tract*. In: Schrier R.W., Gottschalk C.W. eds. *Diseases of the kidney*. 4th ed. Boston: Little Brown, 1015-47, 1988.

[42] MOTT K.E., DIXON H., OSEI-TUTU E., et al.: *Relation between intensity of schistosoma haematobium infection and clinical haematuria and proteinuria*. Lancet, i: 1005-7, 1983.

[43] PETERS A., MAHMOUD A.A.F., WARREN K.S., et al.: *Field studies of a rapid accurate means of quantifying schistosoma haematobium eggs in urine samples*. Bull. World Health Organ., 54: 159-62, 1976.

[44] KROPP K.A., CICHOCKI G.A., BANSAL N.K.: *Enterobius vermicularis (pinworms), introital bacteriology and recurrent urinary tract infection in children*. J. Urol., 120: 480-2, 1978.

Chapter 3

Integration of urinary findings into
a nephrological diagnosis

Urine sediment analysis is an integral, and often the most important, part of the clinical examination of a renal patient. One cannot but agree with the statement that "it is as essential for the nephrologist to look at sediments obtained under standard conditions as for the heart specialist to do his own auscultation". It is important for the clinician to perform the microscopic analysis of urine by himself, because optimal information can only be extracted if the microscopical findings are interpreted in the context of available clinical information. The urinary sediment provides the most valuable information because it is a downstream reflection of upstream events, providing, so to speak, a "liquid renal biopsy".

This section of the book deals with integration of information, i.e., urinary findings, into the overall diagnostic work-up of the renal patient. We shall proceed in three ways:

(i) Provide *diagnostic strategies* for the evaluation of patients with hematuria, with proteinuria, with leucocyturia and/or signs of urinary tract infection.

(ii) Describe *typical patterns* of the *urinary findings* in renal disease, i.e., the nephritic syndrome, the nephrotic syndrome, uncharacteristic urinary abnormalities, urinary tract infection.

(iii) Provide a *synopsis* of the findings in the urinary sediment typical of a given renal disease, e.g., in acute exudative glomerulonephritis, lupus nephritis, diabetic nephropathy etc.

The patient with hematuria

The astute physician will first try to answer the following questions:

Is hematuria really present, i.e., can one exclude admixture of blood by menstruation or artefact (Münchausen syndrome)? Is one dealing with erythrocyturia or is the red color of urine the result of pigmenturia (hemoglobinuria, myoglobinuria, porphyruria), or of the presence of plant pigments (rhubarb, red beets)? *True hematuria can easily be verified by demonstrating erythrocytes by microscopic examination.*

The next question to answer is whether hematuria is due to *extrarenal* causes (e.g., hemorrhagic diathesis), *intrarenal* causes (e.g., glomerulonephritis) or *postrenal* causes (e.g. urological conditions, like tumor, lithiasis, infection, etc.).

The urinary sediment is most helpful in making the distinction between nephrological and urological causes of hematuria. In this regard it is useful to look for cylindruria (granular casts, cell casts and, particularly, erythrocyte casts) and dysmorphic erythrocytes. The demonstration of dysmorphic erythrocytes and erythrocyte casts (or hemoglobin casts) is irrefutable evidence of an intrarenal source of bleeding. Barring bizarre cases of combined pathologies, the demonstration of intrarenal bleeding allows one to dispense with further urological investigations.

Proteinuria is of particular help. If the microhematuric patient excretes more than 1 g protein/24 h, one should suspect the presence of glomerular disease and this is virtually certain if more than 3 g/24 h are excreted, if orthostatic proteinuria has been properly excluded by examination of urine passed during the night. In the patient with macrohematuria, the amount of protein in the urine which can be explained by admixture of blood can be estimated from the urocrit of spun down urine.

Colic and renal pain are not always reliable to differentiate between nephrological and urological causes of hematuria. Even in patients with glomerular bleeding, flank pain may result from distension of the renal capsule or from clot formation in the urinary tract with secondary obstruction.

It is important to ask the patient with hematuria about physical activity. Modest hematuria (and also — not further discussed — hemoglobinuria) is often seen after sports, not only after activities implying physical contact (boxing or soccer) but also after swimming or rowing. As a note of caution, however, it should be mentioned that we have seen patients with glomerulonephritis in whom rowing triggered episodes of macrohematuria. We have also often seen microhematuria in joggers. In some, cystoscopy showed petechiae in the bladder. Physical exercise may also trigger hematuria in a patient with underlying urological abnormalities: we have repeatedly seen hematuria in patients with nephrolithiasis after a tennis or soccer match.

Microhematuria and cylindruria are not uncommon in the febrile patient. It is uncertain whether this is due to subthreshold immune damage to the glomerulus. Urinary abnormalities in a febrile patient should be interpreted with caution.

The investigational strategies are somewhat different for patients with *macrohematuria* or *microhematuria*.

The patient with macrohematuria

When taking the *history* one should proceed according to the following check-list: is macrohematuria painless (renal cell carcinoma, bladder carcinoma, coagulopathy, acute glomerulonephritis), is it accompanied by dysuria (urinary tract infection, bladder carcinoma, tuberculosis, hemorrhagic cystitis), or non-colicky pain (renal cell carcinoma, polycystic kidney disease) or colicky pain (nephrolithiasis, papillary necrosis)?

Does the patient have known renal disease or conditions which could explain macrohematuria, e.g., polycystic kidney disease, trauma? Is there evidence of generalized hemorrhagic diathesis, especially a history of ingestion of anticoagulants or inhibitors of platelet aggregation?

The next step is *ultrasonography coupled with plain X-ray of the abdomen* [1]. These will reveal conditions causing hematuria, e.g., renal stones, renal cell carcinoma, polycystic kidney disease, urinary tract obstruction (this may be secondary to clot formation, though) or bladder disease.

One then proceeds to *urine analysis* (to exclude erythrocyte casts, which are often hard to demonstrate in macrohematuria) and to ancillary studies, e.g., *coagulation tests* to exclude hemorrhagic diathesis.

When this has been done one should immediately proceed to *cystoscopy* while the patient still has macrohematuria, since cystoscopy may enable one to localize the source of bleeding to the kidney involved in patients with unilateral renal disease.

Unilateral bleeding almost always indicates unilateral renal disease. Unilateral renal bleeding does not necessarily exclude bilateral renal disease, however; we saw unilateral bleeding in one patient with biopsy-confirmed IgA glomerulonephritis. With cystoscopy one can document a supravesical origin of hematuria and exclude vesical bleeding.

For uncertain cases, one can administer 10,000 I.U. heparin, i.v., to provoke bleeding and see which side it comes from.

As a rule of thumb, for every patient macrohematuria must considered a sign of tumor when malignancy has not been definitely excluded!! Unless the source of bleeding has been identified by the above procedures, an *intravenous urogram* (or computed tomography scan) is indicated. In rare cases, when angioma is suspected but not detected by *echo-Doppler*, one will have to resort to angiography. Even in the presence of macrohematuria, urinary cytology should be examined to exclude malignancy. Specific filter techniques have become available for separation of erythrocytes and epithelial cells.

The patient with microhematuria

There are some erythrocytes even in the urines of people with no renal disease. The diagnosis of microhematuria must therefore be based upon semiquantitative or quantitative assessments (see page 135).

Minitable

Outline of the work-up of the patient with microhematuria
— Documentation of microhematuria (quantitative or semiquantitative tests) and its constancy (dip stix)
— Examination of urinary sediment
— Patient's history
— Physical examination
— Renal ultrasonography
— Additional tests

When *taking the history*, the following questions should be asked:
— is microhematuria painless?
— is there clinical evidence of a nephritic syndrome (edema, hypertension)?
— does the patient have a history of renal disease?
— does the patient have a sickle cell anemia?
— are there extrarenal signs pointing to some systemic disease, e.g., arthritis, purpura or exanthema, ear-nose-throat or pulmonary disease, hemoptysis, sicca syndrome, Raynaud's phenomenon?
— Is there a history of nephrolithiasis, trauma or surgery (this includes surgery of the urinary tract as well as surgery of neighbouring organs)?
— Is there evidence of hemorrhagic diathesis (epistaxis, menorrhagia, metrorrhagia, excessive bleeding after trauma or surgery)?
— Does the patient take platelet inhibitors?
— Is there a family history of renal (e.g., polycystic kidneys) and more specifically glomerular disease (Alport's syndrome or other glomerulonephritides)? Is there a family history of premature deafness suggestive of Alport's disease?
    — Is there a history of nephrolithiasis?
    — Is there a history of documented hypercalciuria (particularly in children?)
    — Has the patient travelled in tropical countries (schistosomiasis)?

When *examining the patient*, the following findings provide information relevant to the etiology. Genital examination (tuberculosis of epidydimis or spermatic cord in the male? genital bleeding in females?), rectovaginal examination (descensus uteri with cystocele? tumor?), skin inspection (exanthema, purpura?), blood pressure measurement (malignant hypertension? hypertension of renal disease?); pulse rate (renal embolism with atrial fibrillation?); thoracic

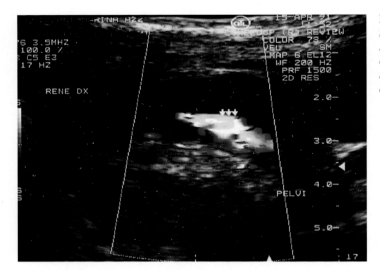

Fig. 3.1 *Arterio-venous fistula of the kidney. Color-flow mapping shows an area of increased vascularization at the cortico-medullary junction (courtesy of doctor Larry Burdick, Milano).*

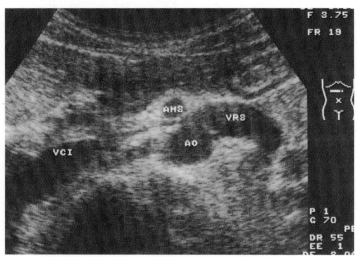

Fig. 3.2 *Nutcracker's phenomenon at ultrasonography. Dilatation of the left renal vein (VRS) due to its is compression between the superior mesenteric artery (AMS) and the aorta (AO) (VCI;inferior vena cava).*

X-ray (pulmonary involvement in systemic disease, e.g. Goodpasture's syndrome, Wegener's granulomatosis, lupus erythematosus [SLE]?); coagulation tests (Quick, platelet counts, bleeding time; only the bleeding time will indicate the patient with v. Willebrand-Jürgen disease!).

In addition to microscopic examination of the sediment, *renal ultrasonography* is the other single most informative procedure. If one suspects glomerulonephritis as a cause of microhematuria, sonography provides information on kidney size, width and echotexture of the parenchyma and echotexture of the medulla. As a rule of thumb, asymmetry of size argues against glomerulonephritis. Large kidneys with echolucent parenchyma and medulla argue for acute glomerulonephritis (or acute exacerbation of chronic GN). Small kidneys, thinning and echodense texture of the parenchyma are more indicative of chronic glomerulonephritis. Sonographic clues that direct the investigation into certain directions are asymmetric kidneys, cysts (primary or secondary cysts of chronic renal disease), tumor, stone, parenchymal calcification or obstruction (one should remember, though, that obstruction may also be the result of hematuria with clot formation). The sensitivity of modern sonographic equipment is such that renal cell carcinoma is unlikely if findings are persistently negative. It is therefore prudent to repeat sonography after several weeks have elapsed. Sonography is *not* sensitive for recognition of uroepithelial carcinoma. (To exclude this diagnosis, cytology, excretory urograms, computed tomography scans and — if indicated — retrograde examination are required; see below). Sonographic evaluation of renal vessels enables one to make the rare diagnosis of arteriovenous malformation (by Doppler echography) and of the nutcracker phenomenon, which is strangulation of the left renal vein between the aorta and the superior mesenteric artery. The two conditions are shown in figures 3.1 and 3.2.

If the diagnosis cannot be made on the basis of the urinary sediment and the above investigations, the following *additional tests* must be considered:

— cystoscopy, urography, computed tomography scan and exfoliative cytology (to exclude uroepithelial carcinoma);
— tests for tuberculosis, Bilharziosis;
— audiometry (if one suspects Alport's syndrome);
— examination of family members (even in non-Alport glomerulonephritis, one will not uncommonly find renal disease in siblings);
— serology to exclude systemic disease (lupus tests, antibasal membrane antibodies, antibodies against the cytoplasm of the neutrophils [ANCA], cryoglobulins, C3 and C4 fractions of complement).

If no apparent cause of microhematuria is found during the first work-up it is advisable to repeat examinations after several weeks, since quite often one will find the cause upon subsequent check-up [2].

Table 3.1 lists some common (in italics) and uncommon causes of hematuria.

Table 3.1 Main causes of hematuria

(i) *Extrarenal causes*

Anticoagulants: Structural causes are found in 50% of macrohematuric episodes in patients taking anticoagulants. Microhematuria is found in 12% of cases when anticoagulation is in the therapeutic range. Other coagulation defects, *platelet inhibitors*, leukemia, polycytemia vera

(ii) *Intrarenal causes*

Glomerulonephritis, glomerular involvement in *systemic disease* (SLE, Schönlein Henoch purpura, Wegener's granulomatosis, microscopic polyarteritis, polyarteritis nodosa, Goodpasture's syndrome, endocarditis lenta), hemolytic uremic syndrome, Alport's syndrome, *benign familial hematuria*, Fabry's disease, nail-patella-syndrome.

Note: microhematuria is *not* typical of diabetic nephropathy and points to coexistent glomerulonephritis.

Vascular causes: malignant hypertension, arterial embolism, cholesterol embolism, renal artery thrombosis, renal artery stenosis (hematuria may originate from ureteral collateral vessels), renal vein thrombosis, intrarenal arteriovenous fistula.

Acute interstitial nephritis: allergic interstitial nephritis, leptospirosis, Hanta virus, acute intrarenal obstruction, (e.g., acute urate nephropathy, high dose methotrexate).

Localized and sundry renal diseases: *renal cell carcinoma*; *polycystic kidney disease* (isolated renal cysts are *not* a common cause of microhematuria);

papillary necrosis (e.g., in analgesic nephropathy); sickle cell anemia (even in individuals with sickle cell trait); renal trauma (occasionally, delayed bleeding); renal cysts; renal angioma (e.g., in Osler's dis ease); medullary sponge kidney or nephrocalcinosis from other causes, (e.g. renal tubular acidosis, renal lymphoma).

(iii) *Postrenal causes*
Pelvic and ureteral stones, uroepithelial carcinoma (papilloma), tuberculosis, hydronephrosis, bacterial infection (rarely, fungal infection), nephroptosis (intermittent venous congestion), Fraley syndrome (hydrocalyx from aberrant artery, usually compressing the upper calyces), pelviureteral obstruction, diverticuli or varicosis of the ureter (e.g., in Ormond's disease, after irradiation), malformation (malrotation or dystopic or ectopic kidneys, horse-shoe-kidneys, duplex forms of renal malformation).

(iv) *Vesical or subvesical causes*
papilloma/carcinoma (vesical carcinoma or infiltrating extravesical carcinoma), postoperative (varicosis, migration of sutures), foreign bodies (needles, grass, wires, particularly in mentally handicapped or sexually abnormal individuals; migration of IUD and pessaries), *inflammation*, i.e., bacterial, tubercular, fungal, protozoan (Bilharziosis); rarely viral, e.g., adenovirus, herpes, varicella; malacoplacia; stone formation (occurs only in the presence of subvesical stenosis); allergic cystitis; interstitial cystitis (Hunner's ulcus); cystopathy after irradiation or cyclophosphamide treatment; trauma and microtrauma, e.g., postcoital, postjogging; cystocele, diverticuli (or pseudodiverticuli in the presence of *subvesical obstruction*; vaginovesical or rectovesical fistulae (after irradiation, necrotizing carcinoma, Crohn's disease); bladder endometriosis (macrohematuria at time of menstruation; microhematuria, occasionally, if the trigonum vesicae undergoes cyclical changes); prostatic hypertrophy; prostatic carcinoma. Urethral disease (specific or non-specific inflammation, trauma, stenosis, foreign body, tumor).

The patient with proteinuria

Urinary *protein excretion* in the healthy subject is less than 150 mg/24 h, but larger amounts may be found even when there is no intrinsic renal disease if there is fever (febrile proteinuria) or cardiac failure or when the subject has been doing strenuous physical exercise, is under emotional stress, exposed to heat, etc. Most of the proteins normally excreted in the urine are of postglomerular origin, e.g., Tamm-Horsfall protein, which is synthesized in the distal nephron. Measurement of specific proteins, particularly albumin, is more sensitive to detect renal disease. The upper limit of *albumin excretion* is 30 mg/24 h. Albuminuria can be diagnosed by dip stix and quantitated by RIA or ELISA. In special cases (suspected insurance fraud, attempts to avoid military service) one should also think of factitious proteinuria. Added foreign proteins can be recognized by immune techniques.

Proteinuria can be diagnosed by testing with sulfosalicylic acid or by dip stix. One must bear in mind, however, that dip stix does not reliably detect light-chains, i.e., Bence Jones protein! Proteinuria can be quantitated colorimetrically by the Biuret method (or its modifications) which quantitates amide bonds. Measurements are best made in 24 h urine collections. Thymol may be added as a preservative, but addition of acid precipitates protein and causes spuriously low values.

When spot urine is evaluated, it is important to keep in mind that at high rates of diuresis, i.e., in dilute urine, tests for protein may be negative despite the presence of significant proteinuria. This can be remedied by measuring protein/creatinine ratios [3] or, more simply, by measuring protein excretion in 24 h urine collections.

In evaluation of a patient with proteinuria one should answer the following questions:

— is contamination excluded, e.g., vaginal discharge (look for vaginal epithelia by microscopy), acute urinary tract infection (which may cause postrenal admixture of protein), or is the test for protein falsely positive (stagnant urine with degradation of urea causes alkaline pH and this gives a false positive dip stix test; several drugs cause false positive Biuret tests)?

— What is the amount of protein (above 1 g/24 h it is suspicious of a glomerular origin of proteinuria and above 3 g/24 h it is virtually diagnostic, at least if orthostatic proteinuria has been excluded by examination of urine passed during the night)?

— Is proteinuria continuous or intermittent? The prognosis of the patient with intermittent proteinuria is much better. Patients with modest proteinuria should test their morning urines with dip stix for some time.

— Is proteinuria an isolated finding (in which case, the renal longterm prognosis tends to be good if there is no Bence Jones protein) or is it accompanied by microhematuria, hypertension and elevated serum creatinine (in which case the renal prognosis must be guarded)?

— Is orthostatic proteinuria excluded? This is particularly common in adolescents. If morning urine produced in the recumbent position during the night, is protein-free, the proteinuria is orthostatic. Follow-up studies over extended periods of time have documented that orthostatic proteinuria does not carry any renal longterm risk [4]. An alternative maneuver to prove orthostatic proteinuria, i.e., the increase of protein excretion during hyperlordosis of the lumbar spine for one hour is less reliable. In patients with glomerular proteinuria, this maneuver will also increase urinary protein excretion.

The single most important examination of a proteinuric patient is microscopic analysis of the urinary sediment. While dysmorphic erythrocytes and the various casts (cellular casts, erythrocyte casts) are highly characteristic of *glomerular disease*, it is important to keep in mind that in certain *extraglomerular renal diseases* (e.g., reflux nephropathy or analgesic nephropathy) and even in cases of severe primary hypertension glomerular lesions may develop, mainly glomerulosclerosis. Such glomerular pathology may produce cellular casts and occasional erythrocytes in the sediment. In reflux nephropathy and analgesic nephropathy, the amount of protein excreted in the urine goes in parallel with renal prognosis. In the patient with diabetes or in the patient with primary hypertension, the amount of albumin or protein in the urine also predicts the coronary risk and is therefore of considerable clinical importance [5, 6].

In the evaluation of proteinuria, the following points are important:

When taking the *history*: when was proteinuria first noted? Was it chance finding, e.g., during physical examination for the army, a health check-up, during pregnancy?

Does the patient have known renal disease, diabetes mellitus or a family history of renal disease? Did he take drugs that might cause proteinuria (non-steroidal antiinflammatory agents, penicillamin, etc.)? Is the patient morbidly obese? Does he have chronic inflammatory diseases which predispose to amyloid, e.g., primary chronic polyarthritis, Crohn's disease, familial Mediterranean fever?

When doing the *physical examination* one should look for generalized edema (pretibial, sacral, eye lid edema), ascites, pleural effusion and hypertension, evidence of thromboembolism. Some rare renal diseases with proteinuria can be recognized on physical examination, e.g., Fabry's disease (angiokeratoma in the bathing trunk area); LCAT disease, i.e., lecithincholesterol acetyltransferase deficiency (corneal opacities); nail patella syndrome (patella defects and iliac horns); amyloidosis (skin infiltration, periocular hemorrhage, macroglossia).

The work-up of the patient with proteinuria is summarized in table 3.2.

Table 3.2 Work-up of the patient with proteinuria

— *History and physical examination*
  Obligatory examinations of blood or urine:
— *Quantitation* of protein (and/or albumin) in spontaneously voided urine (mg/dl) or 24 h urine collection (mg/24 h). Note that in the presence of macrohematuria and pyuria, measurements of urinary protein are unreliable. In the case of borderline proteinuria, repeated measurements (intermittent or constant proteinuria?) and specific measurements of urinary albumin are helpful. In every case of definite proteinuria, it is wise to perform immunoelectrophoresis (or immunofixation) of the urine to exclude monoclonal gammopathies.
— *Urinary sediment* (is there coexistent microhematuria, leukocyturia and cylindruria?)
— *Urinary bacteriology*
— *Serum creatinine*, serum area and, if necessary, endogenous creatinine clearance
— *Renal ultrasonography* (or other imaging procedures, if required)
  Additional studies (depending on clinical circumstances)
— examination of morning urine and test for orthostatic proteinuria
— quantitation of serum proteins (electrophoresis) and serum lipids, if nephrotic syndrome is suspected
— electrophoresis (SDS-PAGE) to differentiate glomerular and tubular proteinuria
— serological tests to exclude lupus (ANF, dsDNA antibodies) or vasculitis (ANCA)
— renal biopsy.

The patient with leucocyturia and/or bacteriuria

Macroscopic evaluation of the urine is notoriously unreliable for the recognition of urinary tract infection. Turbidity of the urine and a visible "knob" upon spinning of the urine may be due to vaginal discharge, vaginal suppositories or precipitation of phosphates and urates upon standing and cooling of the urine. Urate precipitates disappear with warming and phosphates dissolve with acidification of urine. The time-honoured practice of inspecting voided urine for turbidity yields next to no diagnostic information, unless freshly voided urine is promptly worked up by microscopy and is shown to contain abnormal numbers of leucocytes.

Some polymorphonuclear leucocytes are present even in normal urine, so diagnosis of leucocyturia must be based upon semiquantitative or quantitative assessment (see page 135). To avoid contamination of urine with urethral secretions, preputial secretions, vaginal discharge, it is advisable (i) to discard the first urine portion (midstream urine), (ii) to retract the preputium (in males) or spread the labia (in females), and (iii) to cleanse the genitalia prior to voiding. Urine should be examined by microscopy *promptly* after voiding, with minimal delay. This is particularly important if trichomoniasis is suspected from pruritus or foul vaginal discharge, since trichomonads lose their diagnostic motility when coole. According to the criteria outlined on page 31, the (diagnostic) polymorphonuclear leucocytes must be distinguished from lymphocytes, epithelial cells (tubular epithelial cells, transitional cells) or oval fat bodies, etc. Clumping of leucocytes is common in urinary tract infection (figure 2.23). In infected urine, the presence of leucocyte casts points to the presence of renal involvement (and, by definition, to upper urinary tract infection).

In the differential diagnosis of leucocyturia, several possibilities should be considered. When there is fever or after physical exercise, the number of leucocytes in the urine will increase even when there is no bacterial infection. Myalgic flank pain and leucocyturia are frequent in patients with common febrile viral infections. Many diagnoses of alleged febrile "pyelonephritis" are erroneous. On the other hand, weakening of mucosal defenses by viral infection may indeed favor the appearance of urinary tract infection, particularly in females, but this must be proven by bacteriology.

Leucocyturia is not necessarily an indication of urinary tract infection, but may also be seen in cases of sterile renal inflammation, e.g., in lupus nephritis or acute glomerulonephritis. Such sterile leucocyturia is thought to result from complement activation and generation of leucocytotactic factors.

In polycystic kidney disease and nephrolithiasis one often sees leucocyturia without any demonstrable urinary tract infection. The finding of sterile leucocyturia should also make one think of urogenital tuberculosis, a foreign body in the bladder or malignancy of the urinary tract.

Some renal and extrarenal causes of leucocyturia are listed in the table 3.3.

In the evaluation of the adult patient with leucocyturia and suspected urinary tract infection (UTI), the first step is *differentiation* of *lower and upper urinary tract infection*. Points indicative of upper UTI are fever and flank pain, while lower UTI is associated with dysuria, pollakiuria and, if severe, postvoiding suprasymphyseal cramping pain (tenesmus) or macrohematuria. In males, dysuria and leucocyturia are more likely to be due to gonorrheal or non-gonorrheal urethritis than to lower UTI. In the male, UTI is uncommon in the absence of obstruction or neurogenic disorders. But even in females it is wise to exclude genital infections as a cause of leucocyturia, e.g., trichomoniasis, non-specific vaginitis, candidiasis (particularly after hormonal contraception and after antibiotics). Estrogen deficiency often predisposes to urethritis and vaginitis in the elderly female.

Upon *physical examination* one should look for pain over the kidneys on percussion, suprasymphyseal pain and (if indicated) observe the voiding pattern.

Obligatory examinations:
Urinary tests: (coexisting proteinuria, microhematuria, cylindruria?)
Ultrasonography of kidney and bladder (before and after voiding).
Urinary *bacteriology* (midstream urine; dip stix technique). If a positive bacterial culture is obtained one should examine the antibiotic resistance pattern, at least in patients (i) with relapsing UTI and (ii) a suspicion of uncommon microbes. Control tests for the antibiotic sensitivity (Micur test) are helpful. If more than one bacterial species grows on culture, or if grampositive cocci other than staphylococcus epidermidis are found, contamination is likely and the bacterial culture should be repeated with a new urine specimen.

For interpreting urinary bacteriology, it is important to remember that many (female) patients with acute lower urinary tract symptomatology (cystitis) have sterile urine despite leucocyturia. This is thought to result from the bactericidal action of inflammatory products, which are able to elicit an inflammatory response of the mucosa. Consequently, if leucocyturia is present in a female patient with dysuria, urinary tract infection is not excluded by the fact that urine cultures are negative.

On the other hand, false positive results of urine bacteriology are common and are mostly caused by admixture of contaminating vaginal discharge. It is stupid (though unfortunately quite common) to prescribe antibiotics simply because urine bacteriology was positive without having excluded admixture of vaginal epithelial cells by microscopic examination of the urinary sediment.

When contamination has been excluded, a detailed work-up is absolutely necessary for the male patient with symptomatic leucocyturia. In a female patient with a first non-febrile episode of dysuria and no flank pain (i.e., lower urinary tract infection), one may refrain from further investigation when renal and bladder ultrasonography are negative. Some additional studies that may be indicated depending on clinical circumstances are:

— laboratory tests (sedimentation rate; plasma creatinine and urea; quantitation of urinary

protein);
— physical examination. In the male this includes inspection of the genitalia (phimosis, bal-
anitis), palpation of epidydimis and spermatic cord (tuberculosis). In the younger male one
looks for prostatitis (by rectal examination, sonography or fractionated bacteriology),
epidydimitis and spermatic cord pathology (tuberculosis?). In the elderly male one must
exclude prostate adenoma or carcinoma. In the female, a gynecological examination
should be done to exclude introital pathology, cystocele, adnexitis;
— urethral smear and culture and possibly examination of the sexual partner(s) (cultures for
candida and gonococci; mycoplasm by immunofluorescence). If these disorders are suspected on clinical grounds, one may also do cultures for tuberculosis, anaerobes, chlamydia, fungi. In patients who have lived in tropical countries it is also advisable to test for
bilharziasis);
— urological work-up: uroflow, cystoscopy, urography and miction-cystourethrography;
sonography of prostate and lower urinary tract; if indicated calibration of the urethra and
a urethrogram to exclude subvesical stenosis.

Table 3.3 Common causes of leucocyturia (without or with microhematuria)

Renal origin:
upper urinary tract infection (acute or chronic), acute glomerulonephritis (particularly lupus), interstitial
nephritis, reflux nephropathy, analgesic nephropathy, polycystic kidney disease, nephrolithiasis, tuberculosis, medullary sponge kidney, renal abscess formation or pyonephrosis, urinary tract obstruction

Vesical origin:
cystitis, tuberculosis, bladder stone or foreign body, ulcer, Hunner's ulcer in interstitial cystitis, papilloma, carcinoma, bladder diverticulosis, bilharziasis

Urethral and prostatic origin:
urethritis (gonorrheal or non-gonorrheal, infection with sore, herpes, chlamydia, Reiter's syndrome);
prostatitis (acute or chronic); prostatic abscess formation; urethritis with urethral stricture or foreign
bodies; inflammation of accessory glands (glands of Cowper, Littré; seminal vesicles).

Disease of neighbouring organs:
intraabdominal or intrapelvic abscess (e.g., in appendicites, diverticulitis of colon), Crohn's disease, adnexitis, pyosalpinx, pelvic carcinoma, e.g., uterus, rectum, coecum, sigmoid.

Typical constellations of urinary pathology

To work out efficient diagnostic strategies it is useful to categorize urinary findings according
to the following constellations (keeping in mind the possibility of exceptions):
— nephritic syndrome
— nephrotic syndrome
— minor urinary abnormalities
— isolated cylindruria
The glomerulus has few patterns of reaction to injury. Consequently, the urinary changes seen
in glomerular disease are relatively uniform qualitatively.
Disturbed glomerular permselectivity causes proteinuria, which is associated with
(i) cellular casts of desquamated protein-engorged proximal tubular epithelial cells
(ii) granular casts that result from clumps of serum protein entrapped in the cast matrix,
which clumps may or may not be surrounded by lysosomal membranes reflecting origin from
endosomes of proximal tubular cells.

Proteinuria may be selective, i.e., leakage of albumin only, or unselective, i.e., leakage of both albumin and serum proteins of high molecular weight. The distinction can be made by electrophoresi electrophoresis (SDS-PAGE), but electrophoresis is not indispensable and usually adds little of importance to the overall clinical information.

Larger (hypothetical) structural defects of the basement membrane permit passage of blood cells, i.e., leucocytes (attracted by leucocytotactic factors) and erythrocytes. It is thought that erythrocytes originating in the glomerulus undergo changes of shape during permeation into and/or passage along the tubule (dysmorphic erythrocytes) due to the changes in osmolality and to the injurious effects of tubular enzymes.

Nephritic syndrome

In the urines of patient with glomerulonephritis causing nephritic syndrome one commonly finds proteinuria, dysmorphic erythrocyturia, and cellular casts including erythrocyte or hemoglobin casts. These findings reflect to some extent the severity of glomerular inflammation. As a rule of thumb, the more intense the glomerular inflammation the more diverse the types of pathological elements present. One extreme is the "telescope sediment" often seen in lupus nephritis (see page 122), but also in other types of highly "inflammatory" glomerulonephritis. The "telescope sediment" comprises all conceivable pathological elements, i.e., erythrocytes, erythrocyte casts, polymorphonuclear leucocytes, leucocyte casts, epithelial cell and granular casts, oval fat bodies. It is important to remember that the urinary sediment does not permit one to distinguish primary glomerulonephritis from glomerular involvement in systemic disease, e.g., systemic lupus erythematosus or vasculitides such as Wegener's granulomatosis, microscopic polyarteritis, Schönlein Henoch purpura, etc.

In some forms of glomerulonephritis that may wax and wane, e.g., lupus nephritis, increases in urinary abnormalities, particularly erythrocyte casts, are very sensitive indicators of an exacerbation of glomerular disease and may suggest that therapeutic intervention is indicated.

Apart from primary glomerulonephritides and glomerular involvement in systemic disease, the above constellation of urinary findings can also be found in the following diseases:

— hemolytic uremic syndrome
— acute interstitial nephritis with or without systemic signs of hypersensitivity (e.g., drug-induced interstitial nephritis, tubulointerstitial nephritis with uveitis)
— acute renal failure associated with severe infection, e.g., Hanta virus infection (nephropathia epidemica), leptospirosis, legionellosis, toxic shock syndrome
— cholesterol embolism (which may mimic vasculitis, with cutaneous necrosis, hypocomplementemia and eosinophilia)
— chronic septicemia (including endocarditis lenta).

For a patient with nephritic syndrome, one must think of the following possibilities:

Primary glomerulonephritis (GN)
    postinfectious GN
    rapidly progressive GN (particularly pauci-immune GN)
    membranoproliferative GN type I and type II
    mesangial IgA GN

Glomerulonephritis as part of a systemic disease
    systemic lupus erythematosus (SLE)
    Henoch Schönlein purpura
    Wegener's granulomatosis
    microscopic polyarteritis

Goodpasture's syndrome
polychondritis with glomerulonephritis
polyarteritis nodosa and other types of vasculitis, e.g., Churg-Strauss syndrome
To detect an infectious cause (or trigger) of the glomerulonephritis, one should examine the patient for cutaneous infections, particularly erysipelas; tonsillitis and other ear/nose/throat infections; endocarditis. The most important consideration, however, is to exclude rapidly progressive GN (crescentic/necrotizing GN) during the initial examination since this is a treatable form of glomerulonephritis with adverse renal prognosis when treatment is delayed. When this diagnosis is suspected, renal biopsy is indicated, with serological examinations for:
antibasal membrane antibodies,
antinuclear antibodies, anti-dsDNA antibodies, extractable nuclear antibodies,
anti-neutrophil cytoplasmic antibodies (ANCA) including cANCA and pANCA-ELISA,
cryoglobulins,
complement,
streptococcal serology and serology for other infectious diseases, if these are suspected.

Nephrotic syndrome

The term "nephrotic syndrome" is a semantic misnomer. Historically it was adopted on the basis of an erroneous pathogenetic concept of a primary renal degeneration. Today the term may still be clinically useful to categorize those patients with glomerular disease who have heavy proteinuria and little or no evidence of glomerular "inflammation" in the urinary sediment, i.e., few dysmorphic erythrocytes and erythrocyte casts. Proteinuria in the nephrotic range is defined as excretion of more than 3.5 g protein/24 h. In the urinary sediment, the indications of heavy proteinuria include excretion of lipid-laden cells (oval fat bodies), casts containing lipid-laden lysosomes (granular casts with coarse highly refractile granules), birefringent elements (Maltese crosses under polarized light) and cholesterol crystals.
Any disease which causes glomerular damage may also cause a nephrotic syndrome. The more common causes include:
— *Primary glomerular diseases:*
   minimal change glomerulonephritis
   focal segmental glomerulosclerosis,
   extramembranous glomerulonephritis
   membranoproliferative glomerulonephritis
— *glomerulonephritis accompanying carcinoma or lymphoma* (paraneoplastic GN)
— *glomerulonephritis* (usually extramembranous GN) *secondary to drug allergy* (penicillamin, captopril, gold, mercury)
— *glomerulonephritis in systemic disease*
   systemic lupus erythematosus (SLE)
— *glomerular disease other than glomerulonephritis*
   diabetic nephropathy
   amyloidosis
   light chain deposit disease
   renal artery stenosis (rare)
   "benign" nephrosclerosis (rare)

Minor urinary abnormalities

In routine health check-ups, 1-2% of the general population have proteinuria, microhematuria or a combination of both. In postmortem studies, we and others have found glomerular immunedeposits in up to 2% of patients in whom no renal disease had been diagnosed prior to death [7]. The renal prognosis is best for isolated microhematuria, becomes worse when it is combined with proteinuria and is worst for the combination of microhematuria, proteinuria and hypertension. For correct diagnosis, renal biopsy is usually necessary.

The following list gives some of the more frequent causes which one should consider for a patient with minor urinary abonormalities:

IgA glomerulonephritis
extramembranous glomerulonephritis
focal segmental glomerulosclerosis
lupus nephritis (especially class II)
Alport's syndrome
early diabetic nephropathy
residual state after acute glomerulonephritis
myeloma
radiation injury to the kidney
hypertensive injury to the kidney
(secondary) glomerular involvement in reflux nephropathy, analgesic nephropathy, urinary obstruction etc.

Nondescript urinary findings which do not permit any conclusions about the underlying renal pathology are found in several other renal diseases, e.g., polycystic kidney disease, nephrolithiasis, so called "benign" nephrosclerosis, etc. These findings usually include proteinuria (less than 1 g/24 h), excretion of hyaline and cellular casts, minor leucocyturia and non-dysmorphic erythrocyturia.

Isolated cylindruria

The presence of various cylinder forms in the urinary sediment usually parallels the presence of proteinuria. To the nephrologist, the demonstration of casts by microscopy proves the glomerular origin of proteinuria.

In the patient who has recovered from glomerular disease, e.g., from "minimal change glomerulonephritis", or who has latent glomerular disease after a clinically active phase, e.g., IgA glomerulonephritis or systemic lupus erythematosus, cellular casts may be the only pathological urinary finding that persists even when urinary protein excretion no longer exceeds the normal range. It is therefore advisable to examine the urinary sediment even when there is no proteinuria. We wish to emphasize that hyaline cylinders are a normal finding and may be present in the absence of any renal disease.

It is curious (and unexplained) that patients may have massive proteinuria and yet few or no casts. This is seen especially in some patients with diabetic nephropathy or amyloidosis.

Urinary findings in the most common (nephrological) types of renal diseases

The descriptions of the various renal diseases in the following paragraphs are not exhaustive and not meant to be substituted for standard nephrological texts. They are intended to give the non-nephrologist the background needed to interpret urinary findings in patients with renal disease intelligently.

Rapidly progressive glomerulonephritis (RPGN)

Clinical presentation: nephritic sediment and rapidly deteriorating renal function.
Etiology: RPGN may be caused by (i) immunecomplex disease, e.g., systemic lupus erythematosus or membranoproliferative GN, by (ii) antibasal membrane antibodies, e.g., Goodpasture's syndrome, or (iii) it may occur in the absence of immunohistological findings. In the latter case it is presumably mediated largely by cellular mechanisms. This form is normally part of a systemic disease, most often Wegener's granulomatosis or microscopic polyarteritis. It is uncertain whether or not there is an "idiopathic" variety of RPGN, one which is negative for immunohistology and restricted to the kidney. It is suspected that this entity is always part of a vasculitis. The latter forms (iii) can now be recognized by newly identified autoantibodies to cytoplasmic constituents of polymorphonuclear neutrophils (ANCA).
Glomerular pathology: extraglomerular proliferation ("crescents") with severe glomerular necrotizing or exudative lesions (figures 3.3 a, b).
Clinical course: when left untreated, it leads rapidly to irreversible renal failure. Early recognition is crucial, since prompt therapeutic intervention with steroids and cyclophosphamide reverses renal prognosis and may even bring about healing.
Typical urinary findings: the importance of the nephritic urinary sediment in a patient with a recent rise in serum creatinine is that it is usually the first indication of possible glomerulonephritis. The nephritic sediment argues against such other causes as acute tubular necrosis, renal dysfunction from drug toxicity, or elevation of serum creatinine from prerenal causes. When the glomerular lesions heal with appropriate therapy, dysmorphic erythrocytes and erythrocyte casts usually disappear rapidly, but modest proteinuria, approximately 1 g/24 h, and cellular casts may persist without indicating glomerular inflammation. Relapse of the disease may be accompanied by reappearance of a nephritic sediment.

Goodpasture's syndrome

Goodpasture's syndrome results from the presence of cross reacting antibodies against basal glomerular membrane and lung capillary antigens (figure 3.3 c). The syndrome is characterized by rapidly progressive glomerulonephritis, with or without pulmonary hemorrhage. Urinary findings parallel those of RPGN in general and will not be discussed in greater detail here.

Lupus nephritis

Clinical presentation: usually nephritic sediment with or without elevated serum creatinine in a patient who often but not always has extrarenal manifestations of lupus, i.e., dermatitis, arthritis, pleuritis, etc.
Etiology: overproduction of autoantibodies reacting with an antigen that is present in a variety of cell constituents, such as dsDNA, ssDNA, RNA, cardiolipin etc. The glomerular dis-

ease is produced either by *in situ* formation of immunocomplexes (with separate deposition of DNA, which has high affinity to basement membranes and its antibody) or by trapping of circulating immunocomplexes.

Glomerular pathology: mesangial proliferation (type II); focal, segmental mesangial proliferation (type III); diffuse proliferation of endothelial and mesangial cells with or without fibrinoid necrosis (type IV) (figure 3.3 d); membranous lesions, with thickening of capillary walls (type V). Immunohistology usually shows abundant subendothelial or subepithelial deposits and mesangial deposits of immunoglobulins and complement.

Clinical course: renal symptoms may wax and wane. A certain proportion of patients, mostly those with diffusely proliferative GN, progress to endstage renal failure. The renal risk is related to glomerular, vascular and interstitial lesions, indicating chronicity of the process (scarring).

Typical urinary findings: the sediment is useful for recognizing the presence and — within certain limits — the severity of glomerular involvement [8]. In active lupus nephritis the sediment reflects intense inflammatory injury of glomerulus, i.e., a "telescope sediment", comprising leucocytes, leucocyte casts, dysmorphic erythrocytes, erythrocyte casts, oval fat bodies, granular and cellular casts. When the disease is controlled, the former elements usually disappear, but moderate proteinuria (approximately 1 g/24 h) and cellular casts may persist. Reappearance of erythrocyturia and of leucocyte casts may indicate imminent relapse [9].

If a patient has systemic lupus and impaired renal function but not a nephritic sediment, one should consider alternative explanations, e.g., nephrotoxicity from non-steroidal antiinflammatory agents, hemolytic uremic syndrome, etc. In the relatively rare patient with the membranous variety of lupus nephritis, heavy proteinuria and granular and fatty casts may predominate and there may be no dysmorphic erythrocyturia or erythrocyte casts. A change in the character of the sediment with appearance of dysmorphic erythrocytes and erythrocyte casts may indicate a change in the type of glomerular lesions with transition into a diffusely proliferative form [10].

It is extremely important to correctly interpret the absence of "inflammatory" changes of the sediment in a lupus patient in whom one finds a progressive increase in serum creatinine, since this finding usually indicates that progressive renal failure is due to non-immune mechanisms which will not respond to immunosuppression.

Postinfectious glomerulonephritis

Clinical presentation: usually macrohematuria, less often microscopic hematuria, proteinuria around 2 g per day, often hypertension and edema, with or without impaired renal function, in a patient who had had an acute infection, e.g., streptococcal throat infection or erysipelas. Postinfectious (or intrainfectious) GN may also occur when there is chronically persisting inflammation, e.g., endocarditis lenta, tropical diseases like bilharziasis, leprosy etc.

Etiology: glomerular inflammation secondary to glomerular deposition of immunecomplexes.

Glomerular pathology: in the acute phase endocapillary proliferation with exudative lesions throughout the glomerulus.

Clinical course: in children, the renal prognosis is favorable, renal function spontaneously recovers, and hypertension disappears within a few days, while urine abnormalities may disappear only after months or years. In adults, complete clearing up of the urinary findings is less likely and abnormalities persist chronically in many patients. Even patients who apparently recover from the acute episode may subsequently develop proteinuria, hypertension, and renal insufficiency, probably as a consequence of glomerular hypertension and hyperfiltration in remnant nephrons.

Typical urinary findings: in the acute phase, the urinary findings correspond to those of a full-blown nephritic syndrome (see page 119). In patients who go into remission, proteinuria and hematuria usually disappear by the end of the first year, but in some 15% of patients microhematuria, often without erythrocyte casts, may persist for years [11]. Persistence is not necessarily indicative of chronic glomerulonephritis.

Mesangial IgA glomerulonephritis

Clinical presentation: the disease may present either as recurrent episodes of macrohematuria or as persisting urinary abnormalities, i.e., microhematuria and proteinuria in a patient who in the long run may develop hypertension and renal failure. It is the most common type of glomerulonephritis, accounting for approximately 30% of all renal biopsies.

Etiology: the precise etiology of the disorder is unknown, but it is generally thought to be secondary to an abnormality of IgA immunoregulation which is characterized by mesangial deposition of IgA with or without deposits of IgG and complement. It is likely that IgA nephritis is an immune complex disease caused either by an overproduction of polymeric IgA or by a decreased clearance of IgA-containing immune complexes.

Glomerular pathology: mesangial proliferation is the hallmark of the disease. Rarely this lesion may be accompanied by various other pathologies, especially minimal change lesions in one type of patient and extracapillary proliferation in patients with rapidly progressive GN. By immunohistology one can find mesangial deposits of IgA with or without deposits of IgG and complement; in more severe cases, deposits will also be found along glomerular capillaries (figure 3.4 a).

Clinical course: the short-term renal prognosis is usually favorable, but in the long run a sizeable proportion of patients will go into endstage renal failure, i.e., 20-40% after one decade. Poor prognosis is predicted if proteinuria is more than 1 g per day, s-creatinine is elevated at presentation and the biopsy shows severe tubulointerstitial lesions and immune deposits along glomerular capillaries.

Typical urinary findings: during an episode of macrohematuria, usually triggered by an upper respiratory infection, one may see a nephritic syndrome, typically without edema and hypertension, which remits in the course of one to three weeks.

In the interval, one will find dysmorphic erythrocytes, more rarely erythrocyte casts, usually modest proteinuria but almost always cellular casts. It should be noted, however, that "mixed" microhematuria , i.e., isomorphic and dysmorphic eytrocytes in the same proportion, may be the only finding [12, 13]. Urinary findings may completely clear-up despite persistence of immune deposits in the glomerulus.

It is important to recognize the rare cases of superimposition of minimal change lesions upon IgA-GN, since in this case the nephrotic proteinuria responds to steroids. Clinical hallmarks are a nephrotic syndrome with microhematuria [14]. This distinguishes these cases from patients with IgA-GN, crescents and rapidly deteriorating renal function who frequently exhibit a "telescope sediment" and a nephrotic range of proteinuria which does not respond to administration of steroids.

Benign hematuria

Clinical presentation: these patients usually have microhematuria either isolated or accompanied by slight proteinuria. Sometimes they can have macrohematuria. Patients often have siblings or other relatives with the same conditions. The renal prognosis is benign although rare cases of renal insufficiency have been described.

Etiology: although information is incomplete, it is currently thought that many if not all patients have thin glomerular basement membranes (below 250 nm), possibly due to a genetic defect of synthesis of basal membrane matrix.

Glomerular pathology: glomeruli look normal except by electronmicroscopy, which frequently shows thinning of the glomerular basement membranes.

Clinical course: most patients have persisting microhematuria without progression to renal failure. In some cases the disease is punctuated by macrohematuric episodes, which can develop after an infection of the upper respiratory tract.

Typical urinary findings: the patients are examined because of isolated microhematuria, presumably with dysmorphic erythrocytes [15]. The finding of a nephrotic syndrome, high serum creatinine and high blood pressure argues against the diagnosis. Examination of family members is recommended.

Minimal change glomerulonephritis (MCG) — focal segmental glomerulosclerosis (FSGS)

Clinical presentation: MCG is typically a disease of children but may also occur in adults. MCG is a pure nephrotic syndrome, i.e., gross proteinuria without hypertension, hematuria or renal failure. Slowly progressing impairment of renal function and appearance of hypertension are exceptional in MCG, but common in FSGS. This disease affects both children and adults and is considered a variety with adverse renal prognosis. Most cases are "idiopathic", but FSGS may also occur in patients with AIDS, obesity, reflux nephropathy, heroin abuse, etc.

Etiology: while the specific etiology is unknown, it is assumed that the two disorders result from disregulation of cellular immunefunction. This is possibly mediated with formation of an aberrant clone of T cells that overproduce cytokines which increase glomerular permeability. In some patients, genetically predisposed (?), hypercoagulability and hyperlipidemia caused by the nephrotic syndrome may favor the development of sclerotic lesions.

Glomerular pathology: in MCG, glomeruli are normal by light microscopy. In FSGS, focal and segmental scarring (glomerulosclerosis) are seen.

Clinical course: the renal prognosis is usually benign in MCG. Most patients eventually are cured, although this may take many years. Remission of proteinuria can be obtained with a course of high-dose prednisone in most patients, but many of them relapse after the steroid is stopped. A stable remission may be obtained with cytotoxic agents in many cases.

Many patients with FSGS progress to endstage renal failure. Only a minority of patients respond to steroids or cyclophosphamide.

Typical urinary findings: the urine findings are those of the nephrotic syndrome. The presence of a mild microhematuria is more typical of FSGS than of MCG. Any deviation from this pattern is suspicious. For instance, abundant appearance of tubular cells and tubular cell casts may point to superimposition of acute renal failure, which is often the consequence of hypovolemia. Hematuria, pyuria and eosinophiluria accompanied by a rise in serum creatinine may suggest the presence of superimposed acute interstitial nephritis, which is occasionally the result of diuretic treatment [16]. The rapid emergence of hematuria without erythrocyte casts, particularly in the presence of unilateral renal swelling, is suggestive of renal vein thrombosis.

Membranous nephropathy (MN)

Clinical presentation: the patients usually have an isolated nephrotic syndrome, without apparent cause (primary MN) or secondary to lupus, HBV infection, drugs (e.g. penicillamine, gold, captopril) or malignancy (secondary MN). Some 20% of patients have proteinuria below the nephrotic range, i.e., below 3.5 g/24 h.

Etiology: immunocomplex deposits, presumably formed locally along and outside of the glomerular basemement membrane (subepithelial deposits).

Glomerular pathology: deposition of immuneglobulins on the outside of the glomerular basement membrane, accompanied by overabundant formation of basement membrane material. The excess basement membrane material surrounds the immunedeposits and finally leads to diffuse thickening of the basement membrane (figures 3.4 b, c).

Clinical course: this is highly variable, but some 30 to 40% of the patients progress to end-stage renal failure and some others may suffer from thrombotic complications caused by the nephrotic syndrome. The course of the disease can be modified by immunetherapy. Consequently, correct diagnosis by renal biopsy is important.

Typical urinary findings: the urinary findings usually reflect the constellation of the nephrotic syndrome, but mild dysmorphic microhematuria is quite frequent. Membranous nephropathy may precede the onset of serologically overt SLE by years. The presence of abundant hematuria may raise this possibility. Rapid appearance of macrohematuria, with or without unilateral enlargement of the kidney, is suggestive of renal vein thrombosis [17]. Rapid transition into a full blown nephritic sediment ("telescope sediment") accompanied by a rise in serum creatinine, is suggestive of a possible, although rare, transition from membranous to extracapillary proliferative GN [18].

Diabetic nephropathy

Clinical presentation: proteinuria, hypertension and progressive renal failure are part of the late microvascular complications of diabetes mellitus. In the type I diabetic, they occur usually 10-15 years after the onset of the disease. In the type II diabetic (because of uncertainty about the onset of the disease), they occur at variable intervals after diagnosis. Diabetic nephropathy is usually accompanied by diabetic retinopathy.

Etiology: the biochemical mechanisms by which diabetes with hyperglycemia leads to microangiopathy and pathology of the glomerulus (and of the retina) have not been clarified, but a major role of accumulation of advanced glycosylation products is suspected.

Glomerular pathology: the glomeruli have thickening of basement membranes and mesangial expansion. In one form, the mesangial expansion is diffuse by light microscopy, in another the mesangium is expanded by nodules of PAS-positive material (nodular form of Kimmelstiel Wilson's glomerulosclerosis).

Clinical course: in the course of several years, progression to endstage renal failure is virtually certain.

Typical urinary findings: initially one sees only modest selective albuminuria, later marked non-selected proteinuria, and in advanced stages often nephrotic range non-selective proteinuria. The recognition of incipient albuminuria ("microalbuminuria"), i.e. excretion in the range of 30-300 mg/24 h, necessitates the use of specific methods (RIA, ELISA or specific stix). For unknown reasons, the number of casts and cellular elements is often relatively very small in diabetics with heavy proteinuria.

An important question is how leucocyturia, microhematuria and casts should be interpreted in the known presence of diabetes. If the patient has diabetes of long duration and retinopathy, Kimmelstiel Wilson glomerulosclerosis remains the most likely diagnosis. For patients with diabetes mellitus of recent onset, other diagnoses have to be considered, particularly superimposed glomerulonephritis, which is not exceptional. Microhematuria is not a typical feature of diabetes mellitus and should raise suspicion of superimposed GN [19]. Leucocyturia should make one aware of the presence of urinary tract infection (which is more frequent in diabetics). A rare complication of urinary tract infection in diabetics is septic papillary necrosis, which can present with flank pain and macrohematuria. Candidae are frequently found in the urine, and occasionally there is CO_2 formation in the urine by gas-forming E. coli.

Monoclonal gammopathies

Clinical presentation: the patients are usually seen for proteinuria, with or without progressive renal failure. These are usually elderly patients with high sedimentation rates, anemia, asthenia and sometimes skeletal pain due to osteolytic lesions.
Etiology: abnormal immunoglobulins are produced by a clone of pathological B cells. This occurs in myeloma (IgG and IgA isotypes) or in Waldenström's disease (IgM isotype). Occasionally monoclonal gammopathy is also seen in other tumors of the lymphatic series. The diagnosis is made by immunoelectrophoresis or immunofixation of serum and urine and by the bone marrow aspiration. The presence of even a mild hypercalcemia in a patient with renal insufficiency should arouse suspicion of an underlying myeloma.
Renal pathology: monoclonal gammopathies may cause a wide spectrum of renal changes: (i) typical Bence Jones kidney (tubular casts, tubular atrophy), (ii) classical amyloidosis, (iii) glomerular involvement (resembling diabetic glomerulosclerosis) secondary to non-fibrillary deposition of light chains (light chain deposition disease), and (iv) hyaline occlusion of glomerular capillaries with mesangial proliferation seen in monoclonal cryoglobulinemia.
Clinical course: usually progression to renal failure.
Typical urinary findings: the patients usually have heavy proteinuria with granular, cellular casts and lipids. By immunofluorescence, the casts have been shown to consist predominantly of either kappa or lambda light chains [20]. A nephritic sediment with dysmorphic erythrocytes and red cell casts is seen in patients with active monoclonal cryoglobulinemia. The demonstration of amyloid fibrils by electronmicroscopy is unreliable [21]. In occasional patients, myeloma cells have been found in the urinary sediment, i.e., cells with oval to round excentric nuclei with peripheral clumping of nuclear chromatin, prominent nucleoli and a high nucleus/cytoplasm ratio [22]. In sediments of patients with myeloma kidney, myeloma casts, i.e., casts surrounded by syncitial cells, may be found after staining [23].

Acute tubular necrosis

Clinical presentation: acute impairment of renal excretory function (glomerular filtration rate) in the clinical context of
(i) shock, especially septic shock;
(ii) exposure to nephrotoxins, e.g., organic solvents, heavy metals, amanita phalloides, drugs;
(iii) tubular obstruction from exogenous substances, (e.g. drugs like methotrexate) or endogenous substances (e.g. urate, Bence Jones protein, hemoglobin and myoglobin).
Renal pathology: one observes widening of tubules and necrosis of some epithelial cells (only rarely, extensive tubular necrosis), tubular casts and interstitial swelling.
Clinical course: this is a potentially reversible condition. The patient must be tided over the phase of renal insufficiency by one of several dialysis methods.
Typical urinary findings: urine analysis is helpful for differentiating the patient who is in shock without functional renal impairment (usually low urinary Na, high urinary creatinine and high creatinine U/P ratio) from the patient with intrinsic impairment of renal function, which is usually not immediately reversible after correction of the eliciting cause, e.g., hypovolemia or hypotension. In the latter case the urine resembles the primary filtrate, i.e., with

high urinary Na, low urinary creatinine and U/P ratio of creatinine. There is also modest pro-teinuria and excretion of granular and cellular casts, as well as necrotic tubular cells [24]. The salient features of the urinary findings are summarized in the following table:

Distinction between so-called prerenal failure and (organic) acute renal failure.		
	Prerenal failure	Acute renal failure
Urinary Na (mmol/l)	<20	>40
Ratio urine/serum osmolality	>1.3	<1.3
Ratio urine/serum creatinine	>40	<20
Na fractional excretion	<1	>1

In the patient with myoglobinuria and hemoglobinuria, the diagnosis can be made by mea-surements of hemoglobin and myoglobin excretion. The urinary sediment shows no erythro-cytes while the test for occult blood is positive. Pigmented granular casts, similar to hemoglobin casts resulting from renal hematuria may be present in patients with myoglobin-uria [25]. (See figure 2.84)

Acute interstitial nephritis

Clinical presentation: this disease generally results from a hypersensitivity to a drug (more often an antibiotic or a nonsteroidal antiinflammatory drug). After some days the patient pre-sents fever, rash, oliguria, sometimes macrohematuria. Acute interstitial nephritis may also complicate bacterial or viral infection. For some patients no cause can be identified.
Renal pathology: there are interstitial infiltrates with polymorphonuclear leucocytes, eosinophils, mononuclear cells, and occasionally granuloma formation.
Clinical course: if drug is discontinued renal function will improve in most patients. Although the role of corticosteroids is still uncertain, it is reasonable to give a course of high-dose cor-ticosteroids, at least to cases with more severe renal insufficiency. It is extremely important to recognize the patient with acute interstitial nephritis. If this condition is caused by drugs, the patient risks occurrence of permanent renal injury after reexposure. Hints as to renal failure are systemic signs of allergy, such as fever (drug fever) or exanthema.
Typical urinary findings: leucocyturia, particularly eosinophiluria, copious excretion of cel-lular casts and intense microhematuria may indicate the presence of acute interstitial nephri-tis [26]. In the presence of these findings, renal biopsy is indicated to confirm the diagnosis. After rifampicin or penicillin derivatives have been taken, even episodes of macrohematuria may occur. Massive hematuria is also seen in interstitial nephritis caused by Hanta virus in-fection (in this case the diagnosis can be made by serology) as well as in leptospirosis. Red blood cell casts are rare, so that their presence should suggest an alternative diagnosis, e.g. rapidly progressive glomerulonephritis [27]. Although a more than 5% eosinophiluria is typi-cal of acute interstitial nephritis, it is not specific, since it may also be found occasionally in rapidly progressive glomerulonephritis [28].

Renal transplantation

Renal transplantation represents the treatment of choice for most uremic patients. With the available immunosuppression, the graft and patient survivals are excellent both in living donor and cadaveric recipients. Several complications can occur, however, after transplanta-tion. In the early post-transplant period, kidney dysfunction, caused either by acute rejection, tubular necrosis, viral infections or cyclosporine nephrotoxicity, can occur and can pose difficult diagnostic problems. In these instances, the cytological examination of the urinary sediment may be helpful.

Acute rejection may occur at any time, but it is particularly frequent in the first month after transplantation. The clinical presentation is variable. When patients are treated with conventional steroid-azathioprine treatment, fever, oliguria, swelling of the graft and even macrohematuria may occur. With cyclosporin A, the course is often mitigated and the only sign of rejection may be an increase of plasma creatinine which is a very sensitive, but poorly specific, sign of rejection. Differential diagnosis includes acute tubular necrosis, vascular obstruction, ureteral obstruction or fistula, bacterial or viral infections, lymphocele and acute cyclosporine toxicity. The diagnosis is particularly difficult in oliguric patients when some urinary signs (i.e., decrease of urine output, reduction of fractional sodium excretion, proteinuria, urinary sediment changes) are missing.

Etiology: the acute rejection of the allograft is similar to a delayed type of hypersensitivity reaction. Cytotoxic T cells specifically directed against donor antigens are the most important effector cells. However, B cells, natural killers and macrophages may act together.

Renal pathology: in the typical acute rejection, interstitial inflammation predominates, with infiltration of activated lymphocytes, monocytes/macrophages, plasmacells and even polymorphonuclear cells, with or without patchy tubular necrosis (figure 3.4 d). In the most severe cases, there are vascular lesions with intimal proliferation, fibrinoid necrosis of the media and polymorphonuclear cell infiltration.

Clinical course: when promptly diagnosed and appropriately treated (with intravenous steroid pulses, polyclonal or monoclonal antilymphocyte antibodies), acute rejection may be reversed in 80% or more of the cases. Rejections characterized by severe vascular involvement are often irreversible. In several cases rejection may be responsible for only partially reversible lesions which lead to a chronic renal dysfunction. Finally, some patients show repeat rejections which expose to an increased risk of graft lost and/or to severe complications (e.g. infections, peptic ulcer, diabetes mellitus), due to excessive immunosuppression.

Typical urinary findings: several investigators have demonstrated that acute cellular rejection is frequently associated with the occurrence of lymphocyturia or with a sharp increase in pre-existing lymphocytes. May-Grünwald-Giemsa, Prescott's peroxidase-phloxine, ematoxylin-eosin, Papanicolaou's stain as well as prestained slides containing methylen-blue and cresyl-violet-acetate have been used in different studies. Accordingly, also the criteria for defining lymphocyturia varied from one study to the other. For instance, while Firlit et al. [29] considered large lymphocytes showing pyroninophilic features as typical of cellular rejection, others diagnosed acute rejection when there were more than 2 lymphocytes/high power field [30] or a lymphocyturia greater than 20% with polymorphs less than 55% [31]. It is important to retain that in some rejections lymphocyturia can be mild or lymphoid cells can poorly be differentiated from other mononuclear cells, and that occasionally lymphocytes may be increased also in urologic complications. For other investigators, the appearance of a large number of renal tubular cells is a more reliable index of rejection [32], especially when it is associated with oxalate crystals, dirty background, increasing erythrocyturia, mixed cell clusters, lymphocytes and cellular mitoses [33]. However, it should be retained that the specificity of these findings is low, as necrotic tubular cells can be seen also in viral infections, acute tubular necrosis and in cyclosporine toxicity. Enhanced sensitivity and specificity may be obtained with the use of monoclonal antibodies. With this technique, Segasothy et al. [34] found that lymphocyte and tubular cell excretion were significantly increased during acute rejection. Dooper et al. [35] found that T lymphocytes and increased HLA-DR expression on tubular cells indicate rejection with a sensitivity of 95% and specificity of 80%.

In case of post-transplant *tubular necrosis* there is a variable increase in renal tubular cells and frequent granular casts. In *cytomegalovirus infection* there are nuclear inclusions in large cells, with typical "owl-eye" cells, "milkglass" nuclei, sometimes with eosinophilic condensation [33]. Renal tubular cells with enlarged and highly vacuolized cytoplasm may suggest a diagnosis of *cyclosporine toxicity* [36].

Table 3.4 summarizes the most typical urinary sediment findings in the most common diseases of the kidney and of the urinary tract.

Table 3.4 Synopsis of the most typical urinary sediment findings in the most common renal diseases

Glomerulonephritis	
acute	dysmorphic erythrocytes, erythrocyte casts, polymorphonuclear leucocytes, leucocyte casts, granular and epithelial cell casts, waxy casts
chronic	dysmorphic erythrocyturia, occasional erythrocyte casts, granular and waxy casts, broad casts, oval fat bodies (rare), leucocytes, epithelial cell casts
Nephrotic syndrome	fatty casts, oval fat bodies, highly vacuolated or lipid-laden renal tubular epithelial cells, epithelial cell casts, Maltese crosses, (visible or not by light microscopy) associated with casts or cells or else free, cholesterol crystals
Acute interstitial nephritis	microhematuria, occasional erythrocyte casts,- neutrophils, cellular casts, eosinophils
Acute tubular necrosis (ATN)	necrotic or degenerated renal epithelial cells, epithelial cell casts, granular and waxy casts, broad casts, neutrophils, erythrocytes, myoglobin or hemoglobin casts (in myoglobinuric and hemoglobinuric ARF respectively), urate crystals and casts (in acute urate nephropathy)
Acute lower urinary tract infection	numerous neutrophils (often in clumps), bacteria, transitional epithelial cells isomorphic erythrocytes, (lymphocytes, plasma cells)
Acute upper urinary tract infection	the above+leucocyte casts or bacterial casts

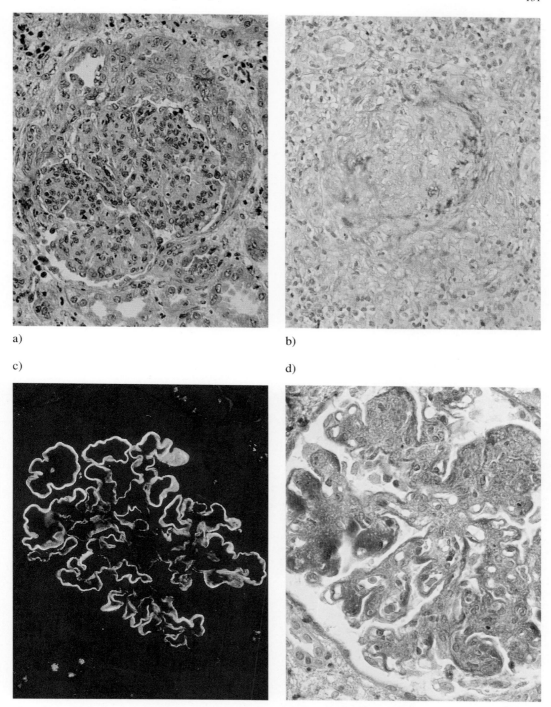

Fig. 3.3 *Pathology of the kidney. a) Rapidly progressive glomerulonephritis (a large cellular crescent occupies almost all the Bowman space); b) Wegener's granulomatosis (periglomerular granuloma); c) Goodpasture's syndrome (linear deposits of IgG along the glomerular capillaries); d) Lupus nephritis (extensive mesangial and subendothelial fuchsinophilic deposits).*

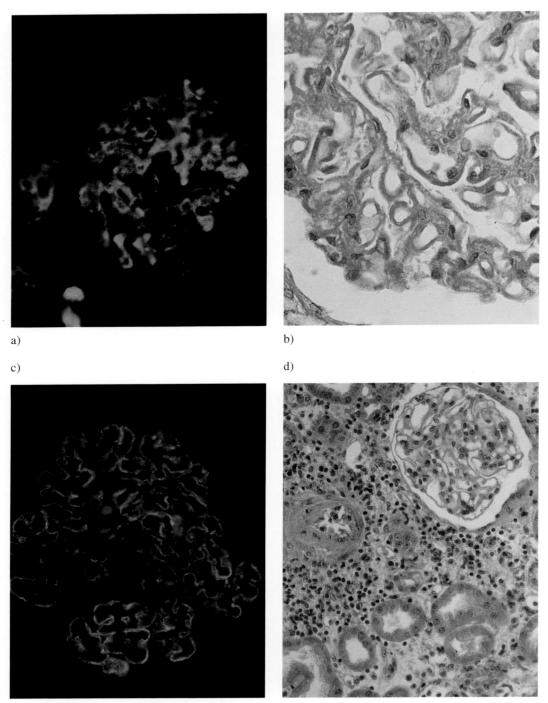

a)

b)

c)

d)

Fig. 3.4 *Pathology of the kidney. a) IgA nephritis (mesangial and parietal deposits of immunoglobulin A); b) Membranous nephropathy (diffuse thickening of the glomerular capillaries and fuchsinophilic deposits in the external membrane); c) Membranous nephropathy (diffuse granular deposits of IgG along the glomerular capillaries); d) Acute cellular rejection (interstitial infiltration by mononuclear cells and edema, with a normal glomerulus).*

References

[1] SPENCER J., LINDSELL D., MASTORAKOU I.: *Ultrasonography compared with intravenous urography in the investigation of adults with haematuria.* Brit. Med. J., 301: 1074-6, 1990.

[2] MURAKAMI S., IGARASHI T., HARA S., et al.: *Strategies for asymptomatic microscopic hematuria: a prospective study of 1,034 patients.* J. Urol., 144: 99-101, 1990.

[3] GINSBERG J.M., CHANG B.S., MATARESE R.A., et al.: *Use of single voided urine samples to estimate quantitative proteinuria.* New Engl. J. Med., 309: 1543-6, 1983.

[4] RYTAND D.A., SPREITER S.: *Prognosis in postural (orthostatic) proteinuria.* New Engl. J. Med., 305: 618-21, 1981.

[5] MATTOCK M.B., KEEN H., VIBERTI G.C., et al.: *Coronary heart disease and albumin excretion rate in type 2 (non-insulin-dependent) diabetic patients.* Diabetologia, 31: 82-7, 1988.

[6] YUDKIN J.S., FORREST R.D., JACKSON C.A.: *Microalbuminuria as a predictor of vascular disease in non-diabetic subjects.* Lancet, 2: 530-3, 1988.

[7] WALDHERR R., RAMBAUSEK M., DUNCKER W.D., et al.: *Frequency of mesangial IgA deposits in a non-selected autopsy series.* Nephrol. Dial. Transplant., 4: 943-6, 1989.

[8] LEAKER B., FAIRLEY K.F., DOWLING J., et al.: *Lupus nephritis: clinical and pathological correlation.* Q. J. Med., 62: 163-79, 1987.

[9] MIDDENDORF D.F., HEBERT L.A., NAHMAN N.S., et al.: *Relationship of urinary red cell (RBC) and/or leukocyte (WBC) casts to renal relapse (RR) in systemic lupus erythemathosus.* JASN, 3: 315 (Abstract), 1992.

[10] BALDWIN D.S., GLUCK M.G., LOWENSTEIN J., et al.: *Lupus nephritis: clinical causes as related to morphological forms and their transitions.* Am. J. Med., 62: 12-30, 1977.

[11] POTTER E.V., LIPSCHULTZ S.A., ABIDH S., et al.: *Twelve to seventeen-year follow-up of patients with post streptococcal acute glomerulonephritis in Trinidad.* New Engl. J. Med., 307: 725-9, 1982.

[12] FAIRLEY K.F., BIRCH D.F.: *Hematuria: A simple method for identifying glomerular bleeding.* Kidney Int, 21: 105-8, 1982.

[13] FASSET R.G., HORGAN B.A., MATHEW T.H.: *Detection of glomerular bleeding by phase-contrast microscopy.* Lancet, 1: 1432-4, 1982.

[14] CLIVE D.M., GALVANECK E.G., SILVA F.G.: *Mesangial immunoglobulin A deposits in minimal change nephrotic cyndrome: A report of an older patient and review of the literature.* Am J Nephrol, 10: 31-6, 1990.

[15] RIZZONI G., BRAGGION F.L, ZACCHELLO G.: *Evaluation of glomerular and nonglomerular hematuria by phase-contrast microscopy.* J Pediatr, 103: 370-4, 1983.

[16] LYONS H., PINN V.W., CORTELL S., et al.: *Allergic interstitial nephritis causing reversible renal failure in 4 patients with idiopathic nephrotic syndrome.* N Engl J Med, 288: 124-8, 1973.

[17] LLACH F.: *Acute reanl vein thrombosis.* In: SCHRIER R.W., GOTTSCHALK C.W., eds. *Diseases of the kidney.* 4th Ed. Boston: Little Brown, 1447-1452, 1988.

[18] KLASSEN J., ELWOOD C., GROSSBERG A., et al.: *Evolution of membranous nephropathy into anti-glomerular-basement-membrane glomerulonephritis.* New Engl. J. Med., 290: 1340, 1974.

[19] O'NEIL W.M., WALLIN J.D., WALKER P.D., et al.: *Hematuria and red cell casts in typical diabetic nephropathy.* Am J Med, 74: 389-95, 1983.

[20] FOGAZZI G.B., POZZI C., PASSERINI P., et al.: *Utility of the immunofluorescence of urine sediment for identifying patients with renal disease due to monoclonal gammopathies.* Am. J. Kidney Dis., 17: 211-7, 1991.

[21] SHIRAHAMA T., SKINNER M., COHEN A.S., et al.: *Uncertain value of urinary sediments in the diagnosis of amyloidosis.* New Engl. J. Med., 297: 821-3, 1977.

[22] PRINGLE J.P., GRAHAM R.C., BERNIER G.M.: *Detection of myeloma cells in the urine sediment.* Blood, 43: 137-43, 1974.

[23] CHESON B.D., DE BELLIS C.C., SCHUMANN G.B., SCHUMANN J.L.: *The urinary myeloma cast. Frequency of detection and clinical correlations in 30 patients with multiple myeloma.* Am. J. Clin. Pathol., 83: 421-5, 1985.

[24] MANDAL A.K., SKLAR A.H., HUDSON J.B.: *Transmission electron microscopy of urinary sediment in human acute renal failure.* Kidney Int., 28: 58-63, 1985.

[25] SINGHAL P., HOROWITZ B., QUINONES M.C., et al.: *Acute renal failure following cocain abuse.* Nephron., 52: 76-8, 1989.

[26] APPEL G.B., NEU H.C.: *The nephrotoxicity of antimicrobial agents.* New Engl. J. Med., 296: 663-70, 1977.

[27] NEILSON E.G.: *Pathogenesis and therapy of interstitial nephritis.* Kidney Int, 35: 1257-71, 1989.

[28] NOLAN CR. III, ANGER M.S., KELLEHER S.P.: *Eosinophiluria, a new method of detection and definition of the clinical spectrum.* New Engl. J. Med., 315: 1516-9, 1986.

[29] FIRLIT C.F., BASHOOR R., KING L.R.: *Early prediction of acute homograft rejection: urinary assay for polyribosomal-rich lymphocytes.* J. Urol., 115: 183-7, 1976.

[30] WILLIAMSON E.P.M., MILLAR R.J., CRIDDLE R.A., et al.: *The differentiation of acute renal allograft rejection and cyclosporine nephrotoxicity by simple urine cytology.* Transplant. Proc., 19: 1785-88, 1987.

[31] SANDOZ P.F., BIELMANN D., MIHATSCH M.J., et al.: *Value of urinary sediment in the diagnosis of interstitial rejection in renal transplants.* Transplantation, 41: 343-8, 1986.

[32] EGGENSPERGER D., SCHEITZER S., FERRIOL E., et al.: *The utility of cytodiagnostic urinalysis for monitoring renal allograft injury.* Am. J. Nephrol., 8: 27-34, 1988.

[33] WINKELMANN M., GRABENSEE B., PFITZER P.: *Differential diagnosis of acute allograft rejection and CMV-infection in renal transplantation by urinary cytology.* Path. Res. Pract., 180: 161-4, 1985.

[34] SEGASOTHY M., BIRCH D.F., FAIRLEY K.F., et al.: *Urine cytologic profile in renal allograft recipients determined by monoclonal antibodies.* Transplantation, 47: 482-7, 1989.

[35] DOOPER I.M., BOGMANN M.J.J.T., HOITSMA A.J., et al.: *Immunocytology of urinary sediments as a method of differentiating acute rejection from other causes of declining renal graft function.* Transplantation, 52: 266-71, 1991.

[36] WINKELMANN M., BIRRIG K.F., KOLDOVSKY U., et al.: *Cyclosporin A-altered renal tubular cells in urinary cytology.* Lancet, 2: 667 (letter), 1985.

Chapter 4

The urinary sediment of the
normal subject

The urine of normal subjects may contain some erythrocytes, polymorphs, and casts. The upper "normal" limits for these elements are not the same for all investigators, in part because of differences in the methods used for urine collection (e.g., timed rather than spot samples), urine handling (e.g., centrifuged rather than uncentrifuged urine), and cell counts (e.g., excreted cells per volume or during a defined time rather than cells per high power field). The different results, moreover, might also be explained by the different criteria used in enrollment of subjects. Because of these differences, *it is extremely important that one knows the upper limits found by the method used for the routine work.*
Quantitative methods, which express the excreted elements per time or volume, are considered more exact than semiquantitative methods. However, very large differences in the upper limits for both erythrocytes and leucocytes have been reported [1].
Semiquantitative methods, which express the number of elements per microscopic field, give more consistent results. Erythrocytes range from "occasional" [2] to about one per high power field [3], while leucocytes range from one to two [3], with the possibility that up to five leucocytes may be found in women [4]. Erythrocytes in urines of normal subjects are usually dysmorphic [5-7], but Fasset et al. [8] have also observed isomorphic erythrocytes.
Using standardized methods for urine collection and handling as well as for microscopy, we found that the urinary sediments of 70 adults of both sexes contained, on the average, 5.8±5.7 erythrocytes (range: 0-26) and 3.1±3.5 (range 0-17) leucocytes in 20 high power fields (X400), without differences between sexes [9]. Therefore, with our method we consider a urinary sediment which contains no more than one erythrocyte per high power field and one leucocyte every two power fields normal. In another series of normal subjects, we found casts in about 70% of cases, ranging from occasional to almost one per low power field. They were almost exclusively of the hyaline variety, although we also saw occasional hyaline-granular and even cell-containing casts. Superficial transitional cells were present in about 60% of subjects, but in small numbers (1 to 7/20 high power field). There were no transitional cells of the deep layers. Renal tubular cells were rare (about 10% of subjects, and no more than 1 cell every 20 high power fields). Mucus was observed in about 90% of individuals, mostly in mild-to-moderate amounts.

Urinary sediment and drugs

Several drugs may influence the urinary sediment findings.
Diuretics: after furosemide or ethacrynic acid numerous hyaline casts may be seen, peaking at 3-6 hours and usually disappearing by 24 h. These casts have no clinical relevance [10]. In acid urine of patients treated with triamterene, granular birefringent casts and brown birefringent crystals may be seen. It is thought that the crystals favor renal stone formation [11]. In some patients treated with hydrochlorothiazide or furosemide, pseudoanisotropic material

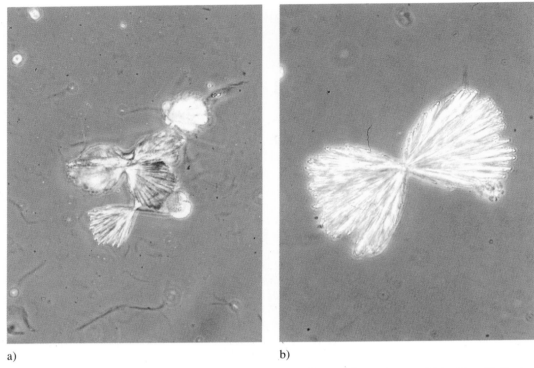

a)   b)

Figure 4.1 *Crystals of sulfadiazine seen in the urinary sediment of a patient treated with sulfadiazine for cerebral toxoplasmosis (a: phase contrast X160; b: phase contrast X400).*

may be seen which resembles free fat [12]. In hematuric patients with glomerulonephritis, loop diuretics cause a transient increase of isomorphic with consequent decrease of the percentage of dysmorphic erythrocytes [13] (see also page 23). Therefore, in a patient with suspected glomerulonephritis and no dysmorphic erythrocytes, urine should be reexamined after the effect of loop diuretics has worn off.

Antimicrobial agents: crystals of various sizes and shapes may appear after administration of sulfonamides (figure 4.1). The crystals may favor renal stone formation [14].

When large doses of ampicillin are given, masses of long needles may be seen in acid urine [15].

Other drugs: all the drugs which cause alkaline urine, e.g. sodium bicarbonate, reduce the number of casts, since Tamm-Horsfall glycoprotein aggregates less at alkaline pH [16]. Conversely, large doses of ammonium exchange resins (or drugs acidifying the urine) give rise to the appearance of large numbers of granular casts as a result of increased acidity and solute concentration in the urine. These casts have no clinical significance [17].

References

[1] GADEHOLT H.: *Quantitative estimation of urinary sediment, with special regard to sources of error.* Brit. Med. J., 1: 1547-9, 1964.

[2] WRIGHT W.T.: *Cells counts in urine.* Arch. Intern. Med., 103: 76-8, 1959.

[3] MILLER R.B.: *Urinalysis.* In: Massry S.G., Glassock R.J., eds. *Textbook of Nephrology.* Second edition. Baltimore: Williams & Wilkins, 1587-609, 1989.

[4] SPENCER E.S., PEDERSEN I.: *Hand atlas of the urinary sediment.* Baltimore, University Press, 18, 1976.

[5] FAIRLEY K.F., BIRCH D.F.: *Hematuria: a simple method for identifying glomerular bleeding.* Kidney Int., 21: 105-8, 1982.

[6] LOH E.H., KENG V.W., WARD P.B.: *Blood cells and red cell morphology in the urine of healthy children.* Clin. Nephrol., 34: 185-7, 1990.

[7] KÖHLER H., WANDEL E., BRUNCK B.: *Acanthocyturia — A characteristic marker for glomerular bleeding.* Kidney Int., 40: 115-20, 1991.

[8] FASSET R.G., HORGAN B.A., MATHEW T.H.: *Detection of glomerular bleeding by phase-contrast microscopy.* Lancet, 1: 1432-4, 1982.

[9] FOGAZZI G.B., PASSERINI P., BAZZI M., et al.: *Use of hig power field in the evaluation of formed elements of urine.* J. Nephrol., 2: 107-12, 1989.

[10] IMHOF P.R., HUSHAK J., SCHUMANN G., et al.: *Excretion of urinary casts after administration of diuretics.* Brit. Med. J., 2: 199-202, 1972.

[11] FAIRLEY K.F., WOO K.T., BIRCH D.F., et al.: *Triamterene-induced crystalluria and cylindruria: clinical and experimental studies.* Clin. Nephrol., 26: 169-73, 1986.

[12] BRADEN L., SANCHEZ P.G., FITZGIBBON J.P., et al.: *Urinary doubly refractile lipid bodies in nonglomerular renal diseases.* Am. J. Kidney Dis., 11: 332-7, 1988.

[13] SCHUETZ E., SCHAEFER R.M., HEIDBREDER E., et al.: *Effect of diuresis on urinary erythrocyte morphology in glomerulonephritis.* Klin. Wochenschr., 63: 575-7, 1985.

[14] HABER M.H.: *The urinary sediment: a textbook atlas.* Chicago: Am. Soc. Clin. Pathol., 52, 1981.

[15] GRAFF L.: *A handbook of routine urinalysis.* Philadelphia: Lippincot, 98, 1983.

[16] McQUEEN E.G., ENGEL G.B.: *Factors determining the aggregation of urinary mucoprotein.* J. Clin. Pathol., 19: 392-6, 1966.

[17] FRIEDMAN I.S., ZUCKERMAN S., COHN T.D.: *The production of urinary casts during the use of cation exchange resins.* Am. J. Med. Sci., 221: 672-7, 1951.

Appendix

Adjustment of the microscope according to Köhler's principle.

To obtain the best visualization of the elements of the urinary sediment, the microscope must be adjusted according to Köhler's principle, as follows:
— Focus on a sample with a low power objective (100X or 160X) (for phase contrast microscopy, shift from the anular condenser to the bright field condenser)
— Lift the condenser up to the highest level and close the field diaphragm
— Center the beam of light through the two knobs of the condenser
— Lower the condenser until the edges of the field diaphragm are sharp
— Open the field diaphragm until it disappears from the microscopic field (to avoid light dispersion, opening should be only slightly larger than the microscopic field)
— For bright field microscopy, the diaphragm of the condenser is then adjusted to achieve the best contrast. For phase contrast microscopy instead, the diaphragm of the condenser is adjusted to the maximal opening and the condenser is turned to the anular position.

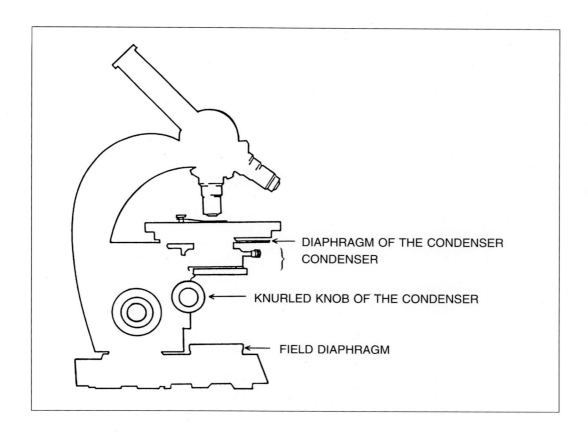

Immunofluorescence of the urinary sediment to detect monoclonal components in the urine
(Fogazzi G.B. et al.: Am. J. Kidney Dis., 17: 211-7, 1991).

— Two 40-ml aliquots of fresh morning urine
— Centrifugation at 2,000 rpm for 10 minutes and removal of the supernatant by suction
— Wash three times in 2.5 ml of phosphate-buffered saline (PBS), pH 7.2. Each washing is followed by centrifugation and removal of the supernatant, as above
— Resuspension of the precipitate with a pipette
— Incubation of resuspended urine for 20 minutes with 100 μl of undiluted polyclonal fluorescein isothiocyanate-conjugated antisera, monospecific for human K and lambda light chains (rabbit anti-human, Dakopatts, Glostrup, Denmark)
— Wash twice in 15 ml PBS. Centrifugation, removal of the supernatant and resuspension of the precipitate as above.
— Transfer to the slide of 50 μl of resuspended urine, which is then covered by a 24×32 mm coverslip
— Analysis of the samples under a microscope equipped for immunofluorescence. Only positive casts or masses up to 20 for each antiserum are scored for intensity (± to +++). The mean immunofluorescence intensity ± SD for each antiserum is calculated, as well as the difference in immunofluorescence intensity between the two light chains (± to +++). A difference equal or greater than + is indicative of monoclonal component in the urine (sensitivity 74%, specifity 100%). The calculation of mean immunofluorescence intensity is made by assigning the values of 0.5 to ±, 1 to +, 1.5 to +/++, 2 to ++, 2.5 to ++/+++, 3 to +++.

Staining of the urinary sediment with May-Grünwald-Giemsa to detect eosinophils, as done in our laboratory.

— Centrifugation of a 10-ml aliquot of urine at 2,000 rpm for 10 minutes
— Removal of 9.5 ml of supernatant urine
— Resuspension of the precipitate
— Addition of 100 μl of resuspended urine to 200 μl of Medium (Flow Laboratories, Irvine, Scotland K A12 SN B)
— Transfer to the cytocentrifuge (Shandon Cytospin 2)
— Cytocentrifugation at 450 rpm for 10 minutes
— Fixation in 100% alcohol for 5 minutes
— Staining with:
   May-Grünwald for 7 minutes
   May-Grünwald (50%)+PBS (50%) for 7 minutes
   Giemsa (30 ml)+PBS (170 ml) for 12 minutes
— Clearing with:
   acetone
   acetone (50%)+xylene (50%)
   xylene
— Mounting in Canadian balsam
Eosinophiluria is diagnosed when more than 5 eosinophils per 100 neutrophils are found. This method also stains lymphocytes.

Suggested readings

— Corwin H.L., Haber M.H.: *The clinical significance of eosinophiluria*. Am. J. Clin. Pathol., 88: 520-2, 1987.
An excellent review of eosinophiluria as a laboratory and clinical problem.
— Fairley K.F., Birch D.: *Hematuria: a simple method for identifying glomerular bleeding*. Kidney Int., 21: 105-8, 1982.
The first paper demonstrating that the source of hematuria can be identified by study of urinary erythrocyte morphology.
— Gadeholt H.: *Quantitative estimation of urinary sediment, with special regards to sources of error*. Brit. Med. J., 1: 1547-9, 1964.
A very instructive demonstration that in urinary sediments the quantitative results can be strongly influenced by trivial methodological errors.
— Gadeholt H.: *Counting of cells in urine. The variability of haemocytometer counts*. Acta Med. Scand., 183: 9-16, 1968.
A study showing that even with counting chambers (hemocytometers) results may be non-reproducible.
— Graff L.: *A handbook of routine urinalysis*. Philadelphia: Lippincott 1983.
Exaustive sections on urinary sediment and on the physico-chemical analysis of the urine.
— Haber M.H.: *The urinary sediment: a textbook atlas*. Chicago: Am. Soc. Clin. Pathol., 1981.
A comprehensive textbook and atlas on urinary sediment. Of special interest, the chapter on the ultrastructure of urinary casts, which summarizes the results of the author in several studies by scanning electronmicroscopy.
— Heintz R., Althof S.: *Das harnsediment*. Stuttgart: Thieme 1989.
A book on urinary sediment, with a detailed chapter on stains.
— Khöler H., Wandel E., Brunck B.: *Acanthocyturia — A characteristic marker for glomerular bleeding*. Kidney Int., 40: 115-20, 1991.
Demonstration that acanthocytes (a subtype of urinary erythrocytes) are reliable markers of glomerular hematuria.
— Kumar S., Muchmore A.: *Tamm-Horsfall protein-uromodulin (1950-1990)*. Kidney Int., 37: 1395-401, 1990.
An updated review on physiology and pathophysiology of Tamm-Horsfall protein, which is the matrix of urinary casts.
— Mandal A.K.: *Assessment of urinary sediment by electron microscopy*. New York: Plenum, 1987.
An entire book devoted to the study of urinary sediment by transmission electronmicroscopy. Of special interest, the chapter on acute renal failure.
— McQueen E.G.: *Composition of urinary casts*. Lancet 1: 397-8, 1966.
The first demonstration that Tamm-Horsfall protein is the matrix of urinary casts.
— Miller R.B.: *Urinalysis*. In: Massry S.G., Glassock R.J., eds. *Textbook of Nephrology*. Second edition. Baltimore: Williams & Wilkins, 1587-609, 1989.
A detailed chapter on urinary sediment. Of special interest, the section concerning urinary sediments in different clinical conditions.
— Nolan C.R. III, Anger M.S., Kelleher S.P.: *Eosinophiluria, a new method of detection and definition of the clinical spectrum*. New Engl. J. Med., 315: 156-9, 1986.
Hansel's stain used to identify urinary eosinophils in various urinary tract diseases.
— Piccoli G., Varese D., Rotunno M.: *Atlas of urinary sediments*. New York: Raven Press 1984.
A textbook and atlas on the urinary sediment, with many and excellent illustrations.
— Roth S., Renner E., Rathert P.: *Microscopic hematuria: advances in identification of glomerular dysmorphic erythrocytes*. J. Urol., 146: 680-4, 1991.
Useful for better understanding of the morphological differences between dysmorphic and isomorphic urinary erythrocytes.
— Rutecki G.J., Goldsmith C., Schreiner G.E.: *Characterization of proteins in urinary casts*. New Engl. J. Med., 284: 1049-52, 1971.

A study which shows that the granules of the casts may be ultrafiltered serum proteins entrapped by the matrix of the casts.

— Sandoz P.F., Bielmann D., Mihatsch M.J., et al.: *Value of urinary sediment in the diagnosis of interstitial rejection in renal transplants*. Transplantation 41: 343-8, 1986.

Demonstrates the usefulness of the study of lymphocyturia in the diagnosis of acute renal rejection.

— Schramek P., Moritsch A., Haschkowitz H., et al.: *In vitro generation of dysmorphic erythrocytes*. Kidney Int., 36: 72-7, 1989.

An important contribution to the understanding of the mechanisms causing the dysmorphism of urinary erythrocytes in glomerular bleeding.

— Segasothy M., Fairley K.F., Birch D.F., et al.: *Immunoperoxidase identification of nucleated cells in urine in glomerular and acute tubular disorders*. Clin. Nephrol., 31: 281-91, 1989.

Study that suggests staining of the urinary sediments with monoclonal antibodies to identify patients with different renal diseases.

— Spencer E.S., Pedersen I.: *Hand atlas of the urinary sediment*. Baltimore: University Park Press, 1976.

A small atlas focused on the advantages of phase contrast microscopy for evaluation of urinary sediments.

— Tomita M., Kitamoto Y., Nakayama M., et al.: *A new morphological classification of urinary erythrocytes for differential diagnosis of glomerular hematuria*. Clin. Nephrol., 37: 84-9, 1992.

A classification of the dysmorphic and isomorphic urinary erythrocytes to avoid subjective interpretations.

Index